Get Strong at Go Series, Volume 1

GET STRONG
AT
THE OPENING

by Richard Bozulich

Kiseido Publishing Company
Tokyo, San Francisco, Amsterdam

Published by
Kiseido Publishing Company
CPO Box 2126
Tokyo, Japan

ISBN 4-906574-51-3

First Printing August 1996
Second Printing February 2005
Printed in Japan

Contents

Preface

The opening (*fuseki*) should be the foundation of all the games you play. If you come out of the opening at a disadvantage, you will have an upward struggle for the rest of the game, no matter how strong you are in the middle-game fighting and in the endgame. This is why professional players usually spend such an extraordinary amount of their allotted time thinking about the first 20 or so moves. Even for them, the opening is the most difficult part of the game to understand. There are so many possible good moves, and no one can say that a certain move is better than another. Unlike the endgame, life-and-death situations, and tesujis, where the result can often be precisely determined, results in the opening are often ambiguous.

Still, the opening is the most enjoyable part of the game to study and to play. You do not have to memorize hundreds of variation as you do in josekis or read out countless possibilities as in a life-and-death situation or in a middle-game fight. You also do not have to make precise calculations as in the endgame. This is all hard and exhausting work. In the opening, precise calculations are impossible, even for the strongest players; what is required is intuition based on good judgment. Within this constraint, you are free to use your creativity to plan your strategy.

The best way to get strong in the opening is to develop a sense of which direction to play your stones. This book, with its 175 problems, will help you accomplish this goal. Most of the first 90 problems are based on four of the most common opening patterns: the *niren-sei*, *sanren-sei*, the Chinese opening, and the Shusaku opening. If you seriously think about these problems and remember the key moves, you will never be at a loss as to how to play in these openings. The last 85 problems are of a more general nature and are presented in order to develop your positional sense in the opening.

When studying this book, it is not important for you get the correct answer to the problems. More important is that you think about the problem, come up with an answer, then compare the correct answer to your answer. The answers are usually only a few moves long, so you do not have to struggle over long and complicated variations. Hence, even if you are only a 20-kyu player, you will be able gain a lot from these problems, and it will also prepare you for the more difficult three volumes on joseki (volumes 2 to 4 of this series).

Finally, I would like to thank the Nihon Ki-in for allowing me to use the problems in this book, all of which were taken from their publications.

Some Important Terms and Concepts

There are a number of Japanese and English terms that are used throughout this book. Each of these terms has a specific meaning in go, and the reader should review them before starting the problem sections. As the reader progresses through the problems, these terms and the concepts they represent will become clearer. I have also used the word 'opening' throughout the book for the Japanese term *fuseki*. This may depart from the usage I have adopted in other volumes of this series.

moyo

A *moyo* is a framework of territory, involving stones extending from the corners to the sides of the board. Some moyos are huge, while others are modest in size. In *Dia. 1*, the four white stones in the upper left form a moyo. The four black stones in the upper right form an even larger moyo, where black has mapped out territory along both sides from his corner enclosure. If Black were to play at 'a' with his next move, he would have mapped out a huge moyo in the upper right quandrant of the board.

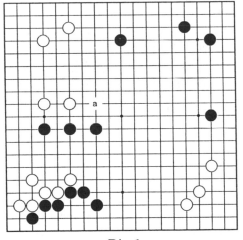

Dia. 1

sabaki

Sabaki is an important concept in go. Sometimes your stones will be outnumbered in one part of the board, so you will not try to make territory there; rather, you simply want to make good shape, rich in eye potential, so that your stones, if attacked, can easily make eyes or be able to escape into the center of the board. In making *sabaki*, it is not unusual to sacrifice some of the stones which are under attack.

light

A light move is one which makes a flexible shape. Moves that make *sabaki* are often referred to as light.

heavy

Stones which are heavy cannot easily make eye shape and are, therefore, vulnerable to attack. If a group of stones ends up as heavy, then these stones have failed to make *sabaki*.

Here is an example illustrating these concepts. In *Dia. 2*, Black has mapped out a moyo at the top. If White wanted to reduce the size of this area, one way he could begin is to probe at 1. If Black blocks at 2, White will cut with 3 in *Dia. 3* and play forcing moves with 5 and 7. What should White do now?

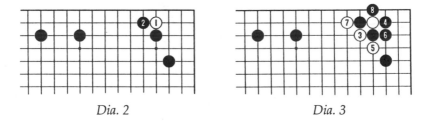

Dia. 2   Dia. 3

The diagonal connection of White 1 in *Dia. 4* looks like an efficient move because it defends the two cutting points at 'a' and 'b'. In spite of this, it is a bad move. Black will peep with 1 and 3 in *Dia. 5* and White is left with a clump of six stones without any eye-making potential after Black 5. These stones are now 'heavy' and will be forced to run away. As they do so, Black will attack, gaining both territory and influence.

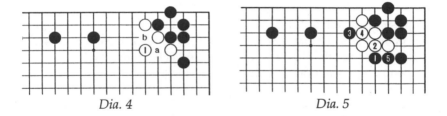

Dia. 4   Dia. 5

Since White 1 in *Dia. 4* results in a heavy shape, it has failed to make *sabaki*. The correct way for White to play is with a 'light' move like 1 in *Dia. 6*. White 1 is called light because it doesn't defend against the cuts at 'a' and 'b'. In other words, it regards the marked stones lightly and is willing to sacrifice them. If Black does cut with 1 in *Dia. 7*, for example, White can make shape with eye-making potential with the moves to 8. With this sequence, we can say 'White has made *sabaki*.'

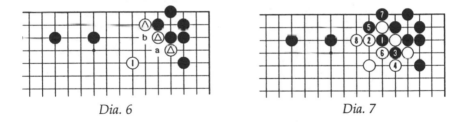

Dia. 6   Dia. 7

Black could also cut at 1 in *Dia. 8*. In this case, White could defend at 2. Black must defend at 3 and White extends to 4. White has driven a wedge between the two black positions at the top. He also has at least one eye at the top with easy access to the center. Again White has made *sabaki*.

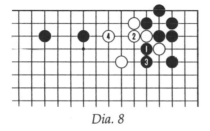

Dia. 8

Instead of 2 in *Dia. 8*, White could atari at 3. This would transpose to the position in *Dia. 7*.

thick

A position is called 'thick' if it has few or no defects; i.e. cutting points. Thick positions are very useful in that they can be effectively used for attacking. On the other hand, a thick position is hard to attack and it is not possible to make *sabaki* against one.

aji

Aji refers to the latent possiblities that exist in a position. Although these possiblities may never be realized, their existence dictates the course of the game and enables certain moves to be made.

In *Dia. 9*, the marked white stone in the corner is dead, but it still has *aji*. Because of this stone's *aji*, White need not fear Black's pushing through at 'a', so he can jump to 1, rescuing his three stones at the top.

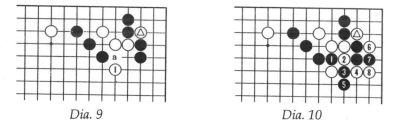

Dia. 9   Dia. 10

If Black does push through and cut with 1 and 3 in *Dia. 10*, White ataris with 4. After Black defends with 5, the *aji* of the marked stone comes to life and White captures Black's stones on the right with 6 and 8.

Introduction

The first 85 problems in this book concentrate on four fuseki patterns: *niren-sei, sanren-sei*, the Chinese opening, and the Shusaku opening. The first three patterns are modern openings which emphasize influence and quick development. The Shusaku opening is an old opening pattern that was thoroughly analysed in the middle of the 19th century. All four are among the most often played openings in professional go and, by studying them, amateurs can master most of the basic principles of opening theory.

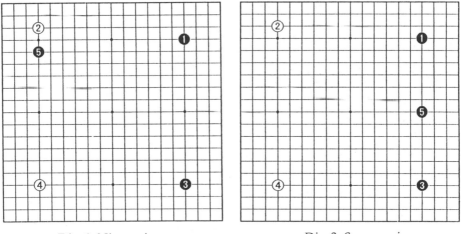

Dia. 1: Niren-sei   Dia. 2: Sanren-sei

The *niren-sei* opening starts with Black occupying two of the corner star points on one side of the board with 1 and 3 in *Dia. 1*. After White 4, Black may then approach one of White's stones on the left side with a move such as 5. Another Black option is to play on the other star point on the right side with 5 in *Dia. 2* to make the *sanren-sei* formation. Black's aim is to make a moyo, but White might play 2 and 4 in such a way as to reduce the effectiveness of a black moyo, so Black might want to play 5 on the left side instead. The popularity of the *niren-sei* has been increasing over the last few years. In 1995 for example, nearly 29% of all professional games started with Black playing the *niren-sei* formation.

The Chinese opening is a relatively new pattern. Chinese players were the first to popularize it in the 1960s (it was actually invented in Japan), and from 1970 it has been one of the most frequently played openings in Japan. In this opening, after playing 1 on the star point in *Dia. 4*, Black plays 3 on the 3–4 point in the lower right corner. There are two version of the Chinese opening: the high and the low. Black 5 is the high version, while Black 5 at A is the low version. Nowadays, the high version is not played as often as the low. Whereas the *sanren-sei* opening emphasizes influence over territory, Black aims for both territory and influence in the Chinese opening.

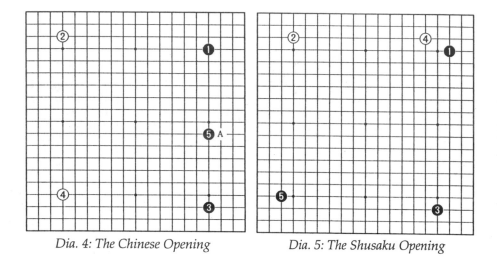

Dia. 4: The Chinese Opening   Dia. 5: The Shusaku Opening

Black 1, 3, and 5 in *Dia. 4* are the famous Shusaku opening. It has been played for more than 150 years, but recently it has been eclipsed by the *niren-sei* and other opening patterns. The reason is that in modern tournament go Black has to give White 5 1/2 points to compensate for his advantage of playing the first move. Without this compensation, it is hard for White to overcome Black's first-move advantage, but with it Black is at a slight disadvantage in this opening, so he must play a bit more aggressively. Studying the Shusaku opening is a good way for beginning players to learn the fundamentals of opening theory.

Problem 1. Black to Play

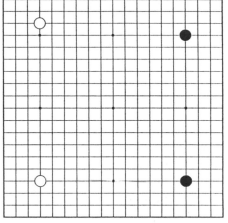

Black has made a *niren-sei* formation on the right. If Black wants to play on the left side, which approach move should he make?

Problem 2. Black to Play

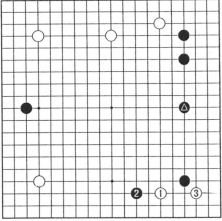

Black has made a *sanren-sei* with the marked stone. Against White 1, the pincer of Black 2 is often played. How does Black answer White 3?

Problem 3. White to Play

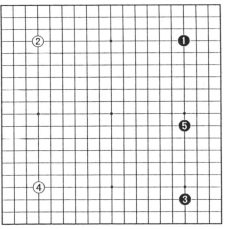

Black has played the high version of the Chinese opening with 5. How should White respond to this move?

Problem 4. Black to Play

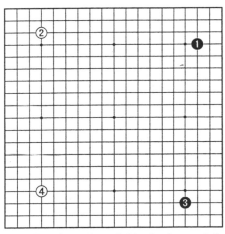

White has played 4 in the lower left corner. What should Black do now?

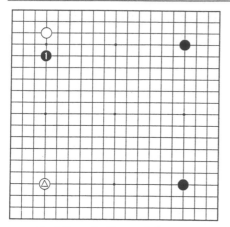

Problem 1. Correct Answer

Black usually plays the one-space high approach move at 1. This move is preferred because White does not have a good pincer against Black 1 in relation to his marked stone in the lower left.

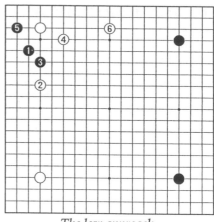

The low approach

If Black plays a low approach with 1, White pincers at 2. If the joseki to White 6 follows, the white stone at 6 reduces the influence of Black's star-point stones on the right.

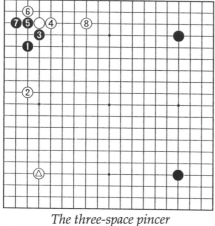

The three-space pincer

The three-space pincer of White 2 is a good extension from White's marked stone below. Black would most likely settle his stones with the sequence to 7, but then White 8 would reduce the influence of Black's star-point stones on the right.

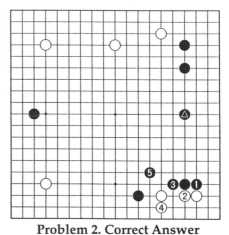

Problem 2. Correct Answer

With the marked stone in the middle of the right side in place, Black 1 is the only move. The sequence to Black 5 is a joseki which is often seen in *sanren-sei* fusekis.

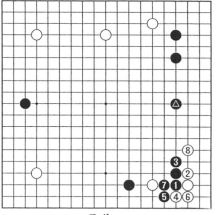

Failure

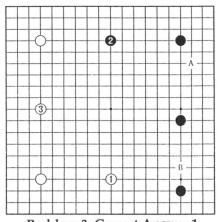

Problem 3. Correct Answer 1

With the marked black stone in place, Black 1 is in the wrong direction. After White 8, the marked stone is misplaced and is not working efficiently.

White 1 and 3 are the standard responses. It is not a good idea for White to play 1 at A or B without any preparatory moves. Whether Black has played the low or the high version of the Chinese opening, White 1 is still the correct move.

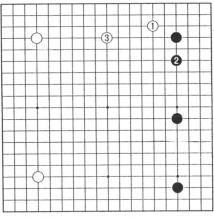

Problem 3. Correct Answer 2

White 1 is also possible. In response, Black will respond with 2. White will then play on the side star point with 3.

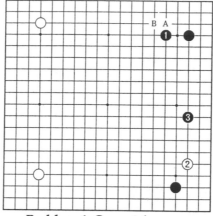

Problem 4. Correct Answer

Black should take this opportunity to make a corner enclosure with 1. Allowing Black to make a second corner enclosure in the lower right corner would give him a large territorial advantage, so White must make an approach move with 2. However, Black can now take the initiative by playing a pincer with 3. This move is also an extension from his corner enclosure above. Instead of 1, making a corner enclosure with A or B would also be a good move.

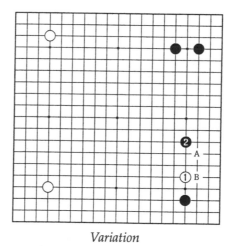

Variation

If White makes a high approach move with 1, Black will play a high two-space pincer with 2 or a pincer at A. Black 2 at B is also possible.

Problem 5. Black to Play

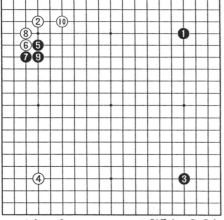

After the sequence to White 8, 9 is the usual way for Black to play. After White settles his position at the top with 10, where should Black play?

Problem 6. Black to Play

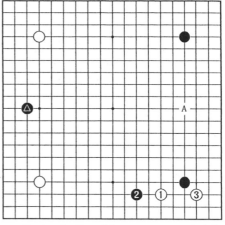

Instead of making a *sanren-sei* at A, Black has played the marked stone. When White plays 3, in which direction should Black block?

Problem 7. Black to Play

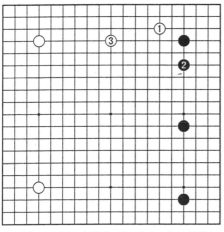

How should Black play after White extends to 3?

Problem 8. White to play

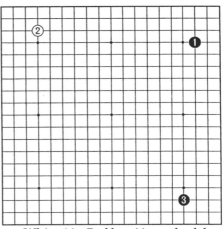

White 4 in *Problem 4* is not bad, but some players prefer not to let Black get the advantage on the right side. What is White's counter strategy?

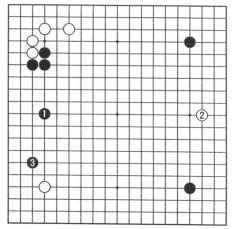

Problem 5. Correct Answer

Black should play the high extension at 1. If White plays 2 on the right side, the approach move at 3 gives Black an ideal position on the left side.

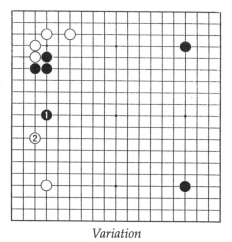

Variation

White could also strike at Black's weak underbelly by extending to 2. Although this seems to be a severe move, Black has adequate countermeasures.

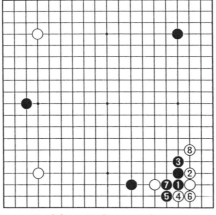

Problem 6. Correct Answer

Blocking from the left side with Black 1 is the correct direction. The sequence to White 8 is a joseki. Even though White has taken profit, Black is happy with his thickness. Moreover, he still retains sente.

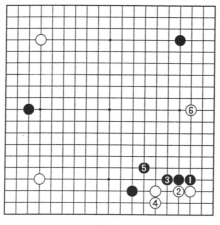

Failure

If Black does not have a stone in the middle of the right side, he should not block from above and play this joseki because White 6 eases the influence of Black's wall below.

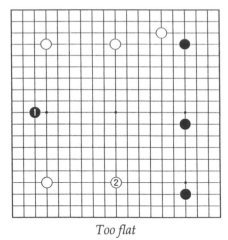

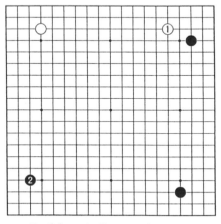

Problem 7. Correct Answer

Black's aim in playing the Chinese opening is both to take territory and to make a moyo. Therefore, Black extends to 1, mapping out a moyo in the lower right.

Too flat

Black 1 is contrary to the spirit of the Chinese opening. White will extend to 2 and Black's formation on the right side is too flat.

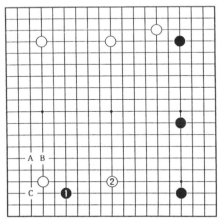

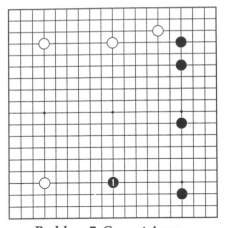

A little unsatisfactory

No one can say that the approach move of Black 1 is bad, but White will pincer with 2 and, whether Black plays at A, B, or C next, he must give up any hope of building a moyo.

Problem 8. Correct Answer

An approach move in the upper left corner with White 1 is a strong move. After that, Black will play in the lower left corner with 2. This pattern is known as the Shusaku opening.

Problem 9. Black to Play

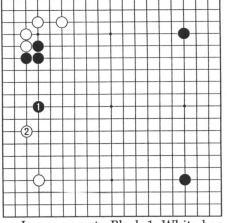

In response to Black 1, White has extended to 2, attacking the weak underbelly of Black's position. With the whole board in mind, where should Black play his next move?

Problem 10. White to Play

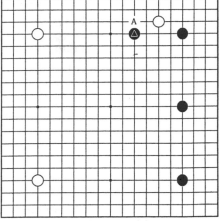

Instead of the usual low pincer at A, Black has pincered on the fourth line with the marked stone. How should White respond?

Problem 11. Black to Play

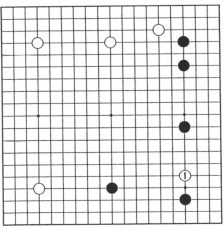

White has played in the middle of Black's moyo with an approach move at 1. How should Black respond?

Problem 12. Black to Play

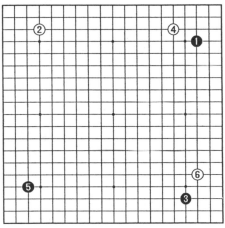

The pattern of Black 1, 3, and 5 is known as the Shusaku opening. After White 6, where should Black play?

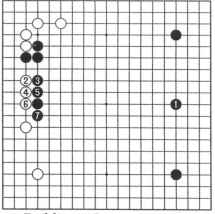

Problem 9. Correct Answer

Instead of defending his stones on the left side, Black makes the *sanren-sei* formation on the right side with 1. Black now welcomes the invasion of White 2 because the thickness he builds with the sequence to 7 works very well with the influence of his three stones on the right.

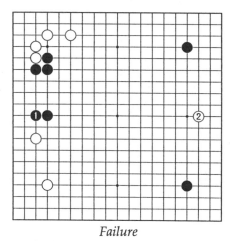

Failure

Black is thinking on a small scale if he defends at 1. White will immediately take the big point on the right side with 2.

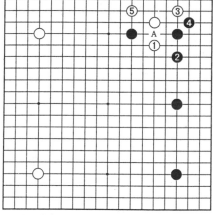

Problem 10. Correct Answer

Black is threatening to shut White out of the center with A. Therefore, jumping to White 1 is essential. After Black 2, White settles his stones with 3 and 5.

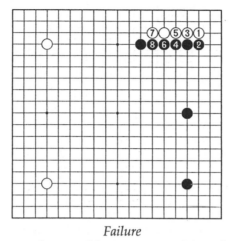

Failure

Invading with 1 may be possible in some positions, but here, with Black's *sanren-sei* formation in place, it is a bad move. Up to 5, Black gets a thick wall without any defects. Compare this with the result when Black makes the low pincer, as in the correct answer to *Problem* 2.

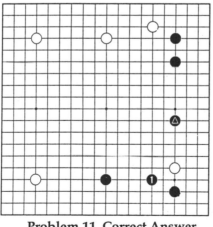

Problem 11. Correct Answer

Black should take the territory at the bottom with the knight's move of 1. This move, in combination with the marked stone, strongly attacks the solitary white stone on the lower right side.

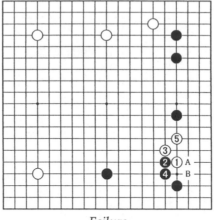

Failure

There is a proverb which advises, 'Don't attach against a weak stone.' Black 2 violates this proverb. Now the white stones, which were previously weak, become strong and Black has no good way to attack them. As you will later see, Black A and Black B are also bad.

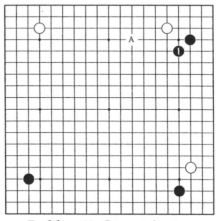

Problem 12. Correct Answer

Black 1 is the famous diagonal move of Honinbo Shusaku. It is a solid move and White will have a hard time equalizing. In Shusaku's time, however, games were played without a *komi*, but today a 5 1/2-point *komi* is given White in compensation for his playing second. For that reason, Black 1 is considered to be a bit passive, so nowadays professionals usually make a pincer around A.

Problem 13. White to Play

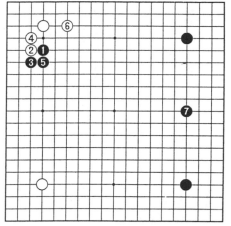

After White 6, Black does not complete the joseki, but rushes to make a *sanren-sei* with 7. What should White do?

Problem 14. Black to Play

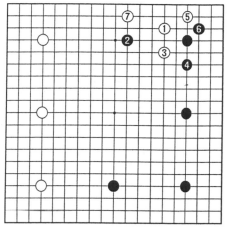

In this *sanren-sei* opening, Black makes a high two-space pincer with 2. The joseki to White 7 follows. Where should Black play next?

Problem 15. Black to play

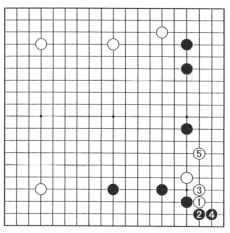

White has staked out a narrow position with the sequence to White 5, a standard joseki in the Chinese opening. What should Black do next?

Problem 16. Black to Play

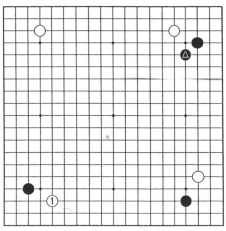

After Black plays the marked stone, the approach move of White 1 is not good. How should Black take advantage of this mistake?

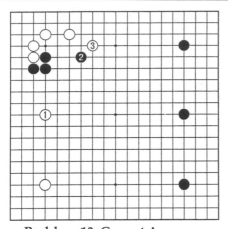

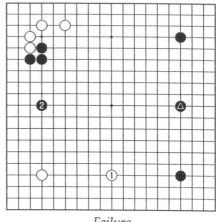

Problem 13. Correct Answer

White should pincer Black's stones with 1 to make them heavy. If Black escapes into the center with 2, White takes profit at the top with 3 while keeping up the pressure on the black stones.

Failure

White 1 is a good move because it erases the influence of Black's *sanrensei*. However, it is bigger to attack the three black stones on the upper left side. Black has now played the important moves of 2 and the marked stone on the right side.

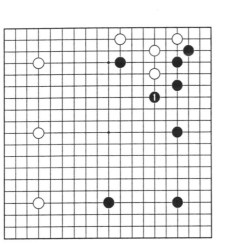

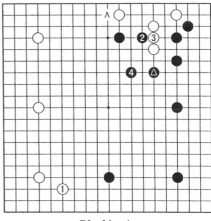

Problem 14. Correct Answer

Capping with Black 1 is absolutely essential. Black has now transformed his *sanren-sei* formation into a large-scale moyo.

Black's aim

If White doesn't respond to the marked stone but plays 1 at the bottom, Black can force with 2, then jump to 4. Black can next aim at A. Black's *sanren-sei* strategy is now a success.

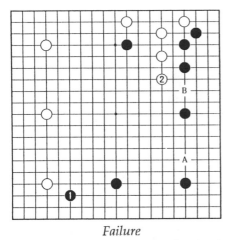

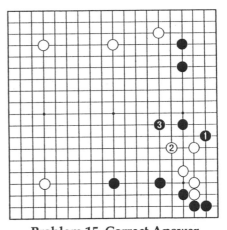

Failure

Problem 15. Correct Answer

Clearly, Black 1 is a good point locally, but White will take the vital point of 2, and Black's stone at the top is drifting in the shadow of White's influence. For the same reason, Black 1 at A is also bad. After 2, White can aim at the invasion of B.

Black should attack the white stones with 1. If White jumps to 2, Black keeps up the pressure with 3, attacking White while building influence towards the top. White's stones are still insecure.

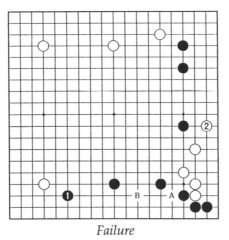

Failure

With respect to the black stones at the bottom, Black 1 is an excellent move, but White will slide to 2, intruding into Black's territory on the upper right while securing a base for his stones. Now that his stones are safe, White can aim at Black's territory at the bottom by attaching at A or invading at B.

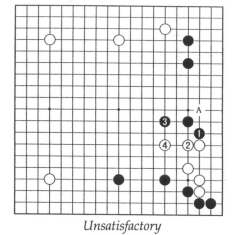

Unsatisfactory

The diagonal attachment of Black 1 is inferior to the correct answer. Not only are White's stones more secure, but White can also aim at the invasion of A.

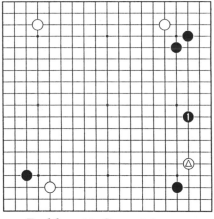

Problem 16. Correct Answer

Black should take this opportunity to pincer the marked white stone with 1. This move also makes a nice extension from Black's two stones above. Black has now taken the initiative on the right side.

Problem 17. Black to Play

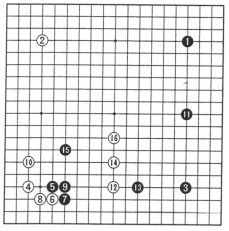

This problem is a bit different from *Problem 13*. After 16, Black's four stones on the left seem to be in trouble. How can Black relieve the pressure on these stones and go on the attack?

Problem 18. Black to Play

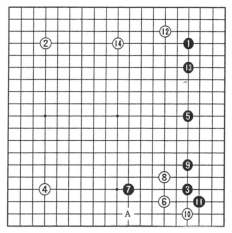

After Black 11, White has neglected to complete the joseki by sliding to A. How should Black punish White for this omission?

Problem 19. Black to Play

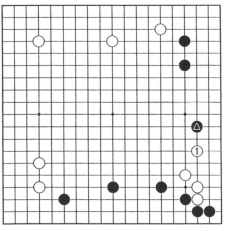

This time Black has played the low Chinese opening. How should Black continue after White 1?

Problem 20. White to Play

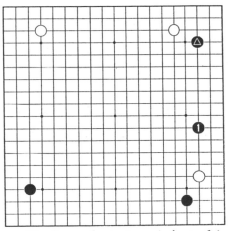

Black neglects to reinforce his marked stone and pincers at 1. How should White counter this mistake?

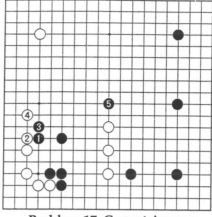

Problem 17. Correct Answer

Black should first play the forcing moves of 1 and 3, strengthening his stones on the left, then cap with 5. It is now the three white stones in in the middle of the lower side that are under attack, caught between the *sanren-sei* formation on the right and Black's strengthened position on the left.

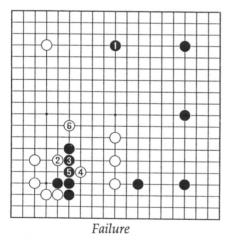

Failure

If Black neglects to strengthen his stones on the left and plays a big point at 1 instead, White will force with 2 and 4, then cap with 6. Black's stones are now in trouble.

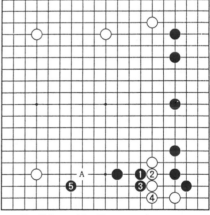

Problem 18. Correct Answer

Black should peep with 1 and rob White of his eye shape with 3. If White descends to 4, Black will take up a position at the bottom by extending to 5. If White 4 at A, Black will hane at 4, leaving the white stones eyeless and under a severe attack.

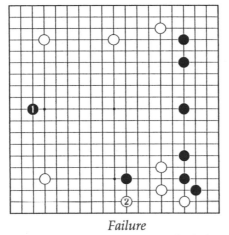

Failure

Black would like to establish a presence on the left side by playing at 1, but White would then be able to settle his stones at the bottom by sliding to 2.

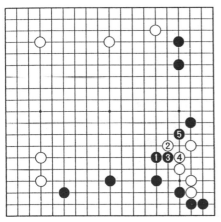

Problem 19. Correct Answer

Jumping to 1 is Black's best move. White will jump out into the center with 2, but Black will harrass White by forcing with 3 and peeping at 5.

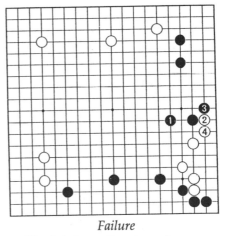

Failure

Black 1 doesn't put much pressure on White. White will play 2 and 4, easily securing a base for his stones on the right side.

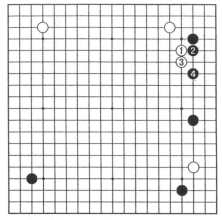

Problem 20. Correct Answer

White should press Black with 1 and 3. Black's position on the right side is now rather flat.

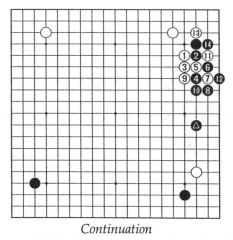

Continuation

White can continue with the forcing sequence from 5 to 13. The marked black stone is now too close to his thick position above, so his stones are overconcentrated.

Problem 21. Black to Play

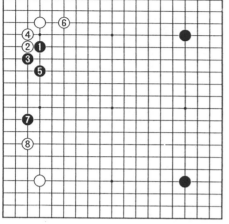

If Black plays the joseki to 7, how should he respond to White 8?

Problem 22. Black to Play

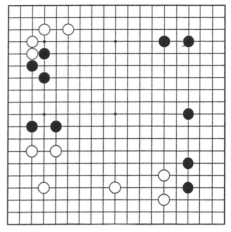

This game has become a contest of moyos. Where should Black play?

Problem 23. White to Play

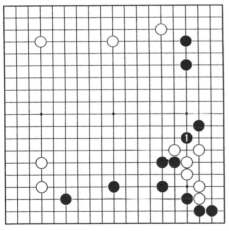

There is a proverb which says 'Only a fool neglects to connect against a peep.' But what about in this case? Should White connect against the peep of Black 1 or is there something else he should do?

Problem 24. White to Play

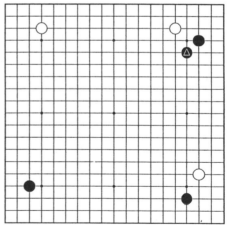

After Black has played the marked stone, what should White do?

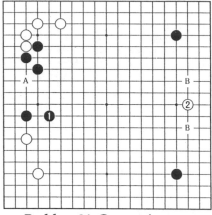

Problem 21. Correct Answer

White is threatening to invade at A, so Black should defend his position on the left side by jumping to 1. White would then invade at 2. From this position, Black would play one of the points marked B and a joseki which involves the whole right side would be put in motion. (See *Get Strong at Joseki 3*, Joseki 9.)

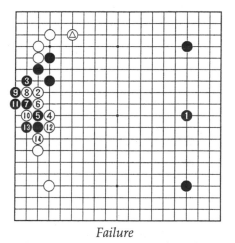

Failure

It is tempting to make a *sanren-sei* on the right side with 1, but in that case White would invade at 2 and make thickness with the sequence to 14. This thickness and White's marked stone now serve to diminish the power of the *sanren-sei* formation on the right side.

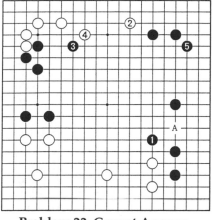

Problem 22. Correct Answer

Black 1 is the focal point of the white and black moyos, expanding Black's moyo and reducing White's. Moreover, this move defends against a white invasion at A. White 2 is the last big point, but Black finishes up the fuseki with 3 and 5, solidifying his moyos on the left and the right.

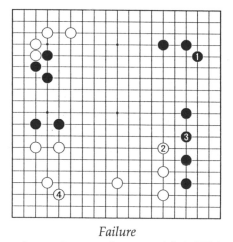

Failure

If Black rushes to take territory at the top with 1, White will exchange 2 for Black 3, then solidify his moyo with 4. The scale of White's moyo is now quite satisfactory.

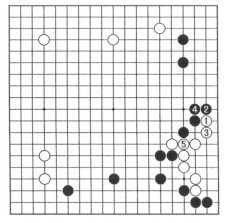

Problem 23. Correct Answer

Connecting at 5 is certainly an important move, but before doing so, White should play 1 and 3, then connect at 5. In this way, White creates a base for his stones and Black's subsequent attack against them will not be so severe.

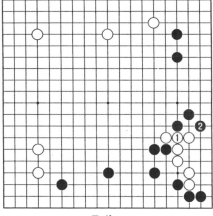

Failure

Blindly following the proverb by connecting at 1 is bad. Black plays 2 and White's stones are rootless, so they will have to run away into the center.

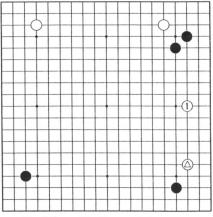

Problem 24. Correct Answer

White should extend along the right side with 1 to reinforce his marked stone and prevent it from being pincered.

Problem 25. Black to Play

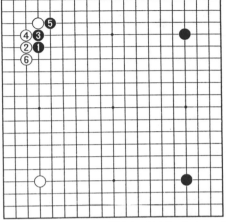

In response to White 2, Black 3 and 5 are large-scale strategic moves which work well with Black's *niren-sei* on the right. What should Black do after White 6?

Problem 26. Black to Play

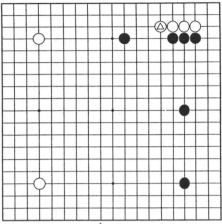

White has just played the marked stone. Taking into account his *sanren-sei* formation on the right side, where should Black play next?

Problem 27. Black to Play

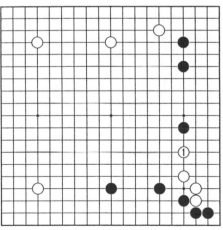

This time White has tried a different tack by jumping along the fourth line with 1. What should Black do?

Problem 28. Black to Play

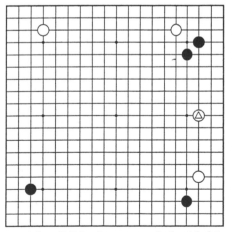

After White has extended with his marked stone, what should Black do?

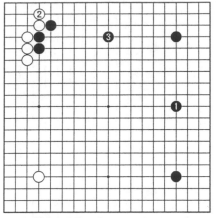

Problem 25. Correct Answer

Making a *sanren-sei* on the right side with 1 is strategically the most interesting move. If White fortifies his corner territory with 2, Black will take another star point at the top with 3. (See *Get Strong at Joseki 1*, Problems 102 and 105.)

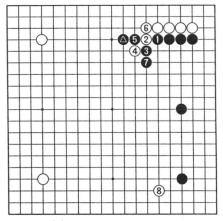

Problem 26. Correct Answer

There is no other move for Black except to block at 1. Confining White to the top is absolutely essential in the *sanren-sei* strategy. White resists with 2 and 4 to get some *aji* in the center. With Black 7, the joseki comes to a pause. White 8 is now the most natural move.

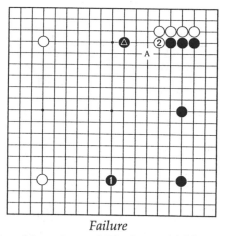

Failure

Black 1 is certainly a big point and Black would like to play there first, but White will turn at 2 and the marked stone at the top will be isolated from its allies on the right. Moreover, the three black stones to the right of 2 are now heavy because they are short of liberties. Black 1 at A is in the right direction, but it is not as tight a move as 1 in the correct answer.

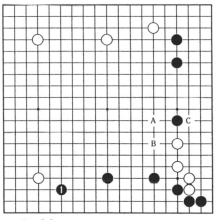

Problem 27. Correct Answer

Black doesn't really have a convincing attack against the four white stones on the right. If he jumps to A, White will follow him out by jumping to B. Black's best move is to make an 'iron pillar' at C. However, White doesn't have any convincing moves here either. Therefore, it is best for Black to leave the situation as it is and switch to the left side by approaching with Black 1.

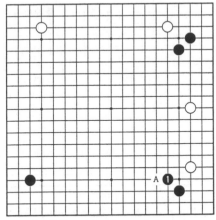

Problem 28. Correct Answer

Black should play another diagonal move with 1 or play the knight's move at A.

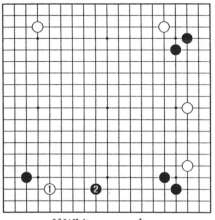

If White approaches

White would like to approach with 1, but, if he does, Black will play 2, which is both a pincer and an extension.

Problem 29. White to Play

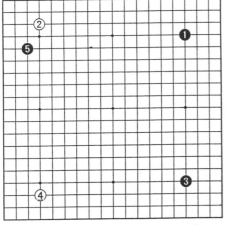

The formation of White 2 and 4 is known as *mukai-komoku* (opposing *komoku*). Black 5 is not necessarily bad, but White can get the initiative on the left side. How should he play?

Problem 30. Black to Play

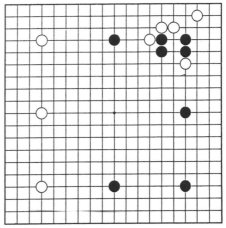

Black has made a *sanren-sei* on the right side and occupied both star points in the middle of the upper and lower sides. What is Black's best move in this position?

Problem 31. Black to Play

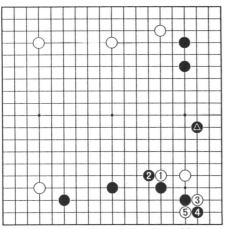

Black has played the low Chinese opening with the marked stone. How should Black respond to White 5?

Problem 32. White to Play

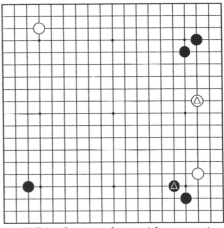

White has made a wide extension with his marked stone. How should he respond to Black's marked stone?

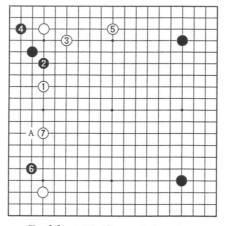

Problem 29. Correct Answer

White should pincer around 1, play out the joseki, and let Black approach again at the bottom with 6. Now White can pincer again with 7 (or A), but this time, besides being a pincer, it is also an extension from his stone at 1. White is satisfied with this result.

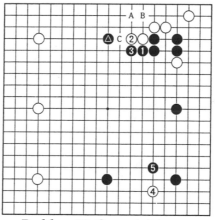

Problem 30. Correct Answer

Black should push along the fifth line, forcing White in the direction of his marked stone. All of Black's stones are now working together harmoniously. If White 2, Black continues to press White with 3. If White next approaches with 4, Black 5 builds a magnificent moyo on the right side. Moreover, Black still threatens White with the sequence Black A–White B–Black C.

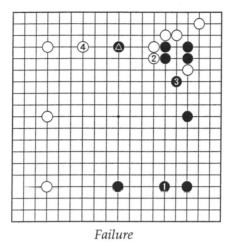

Failure

If Black plays somewhere else, such as at 1, White will seize the initiative at the top with 2 and 4. The marked black stone is now under a severe attack.

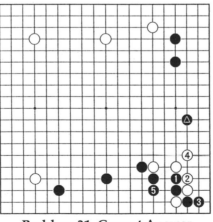

Problem 31. Correct Answer

With the marked stone on the third line in place, bumping against the white stone with Black 1 is the best move. The sequence to Black 5 is now inevitable, and White's group is still under attack.

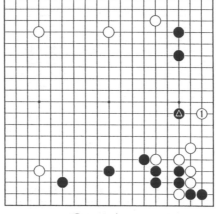

Comparison

If Black had played the high Chinese opening with the marked stone, White could easily settle his group by sliding to 1.

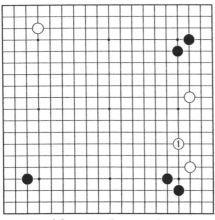

Problem 32. Correct Answer

White should play the knight's move of 1, reinforcing his position on the right side.

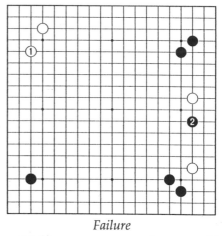

Failure

Making a corner enclosure with White 1 gives Black the chance to invade at 2.

Problem 33. Black to Play

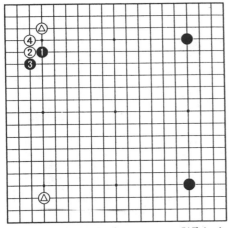

This time Black counters White's *mukai-komoku* formation (the marked stones) with a high approach move at 1. After exchanging 3 for 4, what should Black do?

Problem 34. Black to Play

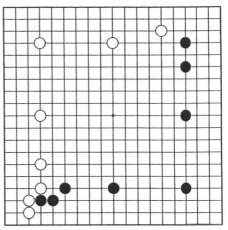

Both sides have occupied all the star points. Where should Black play next?

Problem 35. Black to Play

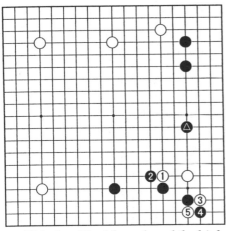

This time Black has played the high Chinese opening. How should Black counter White's attempt to make *sabaki* with the sequence to 5?

Problem 36. Black to Play

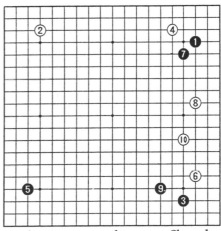

This is a game between Shusaku (Black) and his teacher Honinbo Shuwa. After White 10, where do you think Shusaku played?

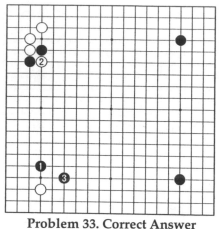

Problem 33. Correct Answer

Black should play another high approach move with 1. It would be natural for White to cut at 2, but then 3 would give Black wonderful influence in the center which combines well with his *niren-sei* formation on the right.

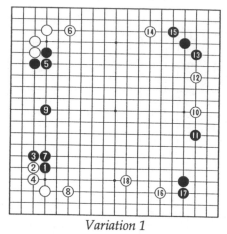

Variation 1

White could also attach at 2. The sequence to White 8 would then be the natural flow. However, Black 9 becomes an excellent move, making an ideal extension from his stones at the top and the bottom. White would then play 10 on the right side. The sequence to 18 is from a game between Takagawa (Black) and Sakata.

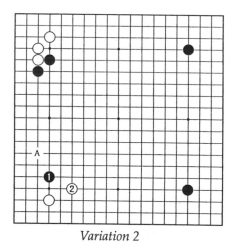

Variation 2

White could also respond to Black 1 with 2 or a pincer at A.

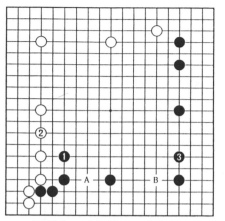

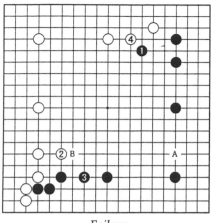

Problem 34. Correct Answer

White A is a good invasion point, so Black should defend by jumping to 1, expanding his moyo at the expense of White's, and aim to invade at 2. White has many ways to respond, but if he defends with 2, Black will strengthen his moyo with 3 or B.

Failure

If Black played 1 in the upper right, White 2 would force Black to defend at 3. If Black 1 at A, White will jump to 2 or B.

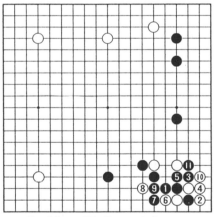

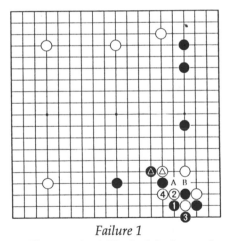

Problem 35. Correct Answer

Drawing back with 1 is a powerful move here. The sequence to Black 11 will follow. Black gets a thick position in the center, while White gets some territory in the corner.

Failure 1

The atari of Black 1 is just what White wants. White will respond with 2 and 4. If Black next plays A, White plays B. The exchange of the marked stones has now become bad for Black.

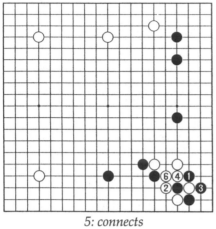

5: connects
Failure 2

Playing atari from the other side with Black 1 is also bad. After the sequence to White 6, Black's moyo has been ripped apart.

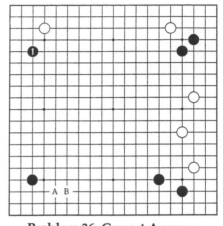

Problem 36. Correct Answer

Black made an approach move at 1. It might seem that making a corner enclosure at A or B would also be good, but Black preferred to let White make an approach move there.

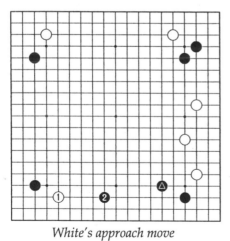

White's approach move

Against White 1, the pincer of Black 2 makes an ideal extension from his marked stone on the right.

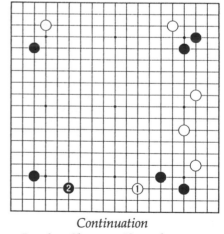

Continuation

In the Shuwa–Shusaku game, White played 1 and Black made a corner enclosure with 2.

Problem 37. Black to Play

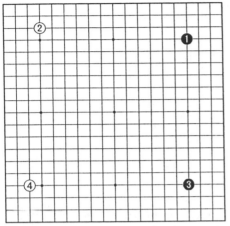

When White makes this *komoku* formation on the left side with 2 and 4, from which side should Black approach?

Problem 38. White to Play

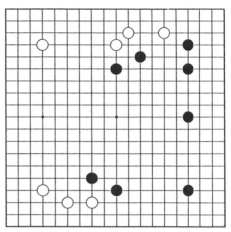

Black has mapped out a vast moyo. White has to prevent Black from solidifying it. Where should he play?

Problem 39. White to Play

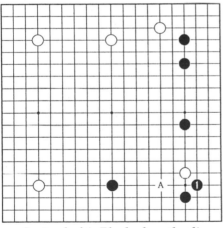

Instead of A, Black plays the diagonal move of 1. As we mentioned in *Problem 11*, this is not a good move because Black's stones become heavy. How should White respond?

Problem 40. White to Play

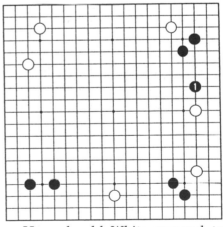

How should White respond to Black 1?

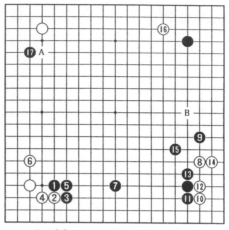

Problem 37. Correct Answer

The high approach of Black 1 in the lower left corner works best with Black's *niren-sei* formation on the right. If the joseki to White 6 is played, Black makes an ideal extension to 7 at the bottom. A corner enclosure at White A would now seem natural, but Black would make a *sanren-sei* with B, so White plays 8 to prevent this. Still, Black gets a moyo at the bottom when he plays 15.

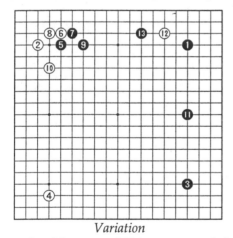

Variation

In this game, White answered 9 with 10, so Black switched to the right side, making a *sanren-sei* with 11. White then approached with 12, but Black 13 became an ideal move, being both a pincer and an extension from his stones on the left.

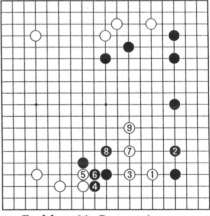

Problem 38. Correct Answer

White should play the high approach move with 1. Black 2 is the natural response, but now White 3 threatens to link up with its allies on the left, so Black must play 4 and 6. White can now move out into the center in good style with 7 and 9.

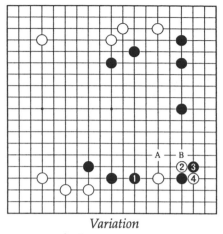

Variation

Black might pincer with 1. If White answers by jumping to A, Black will jump to B and White's two stones will be in trouble, floundering in the middle of Black's moyo without a base. Therefore, White attaches with 2. If Black 3, White crosscuts with 4 to make *sabaki*.

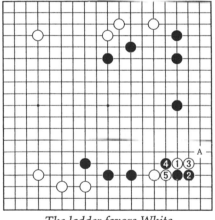

The ladder favors White

Black could respond to White's attachment by extending to 2 and White will not be able to make *sabaki*. If White 3 at 4, Black A puts White on the spot. Therefore, White plays 3 and, if Black 4, White cuts with 5. Since the ladder is in White's favor, he can fight in this position.

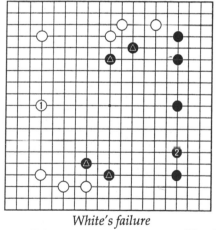

White's failure

White 1 is too passive. Black strengthens his position with 2 and, because of the presence of the four marked stones, White will find it hard to reduce the scale of Black's moyo. Therefore, White must invade the bottom right before Black has a chance to reinforce his moyo with 2.

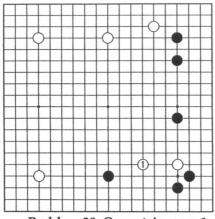

Problem 39. Correct Answer 1

The two-space jump of White 1 is a light move. Whenever you play near your opponent's strong stones, playing lightly is an iron rule.

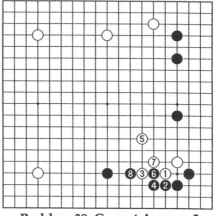

Problem 39. Correct Answer 2

The diagonal move of White 1 is also a strong move. Against Black 2, White plays lightly with 3 and 5. Note the tesuji of Black 6 and 8. In any case, White should not be unhappy, since he has forced Black to crawl along the third line.

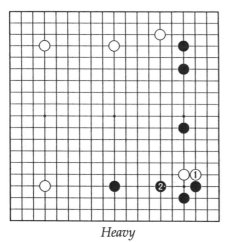

Heavy

White gets a heavy shape if he plays 1. After Black 2, his two stones will come under a severe attack.

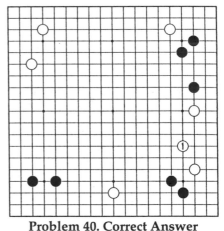

Problem 40. Correct Answer

It should be obvious that White has to defend his position on the right side with 1.

Problem 41. Black to Play

Problem 42. Black to Play

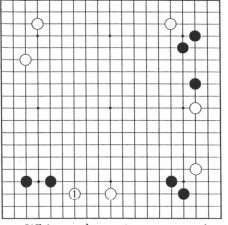

White makes a two-space extension with 1. What should Black do
now?

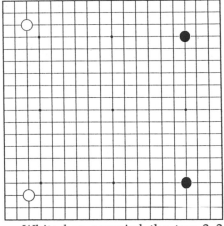

White has occupied the two 3–3
points on the left side. How should
Black play in this position?

Problem 43. Black to Play

Problem 44. Black to Play

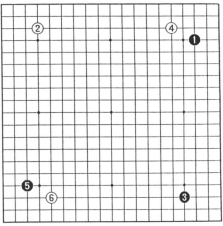

White 1 is a good move because it
is light and aims to make *sabaki*. Black,
however, must not play passively. Instead, he must pursue White persist-
enly. Where should he play?

How should Black respond to the
approach move of White 6 in the lower
left corner?

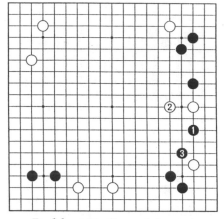

Problem 41. Correct Answer

Black should take this opportunity to invade White's thin position on the side with 1. If White jumps to 2, Black will play 3, and the lone white stone on the lower right side is in trouble.

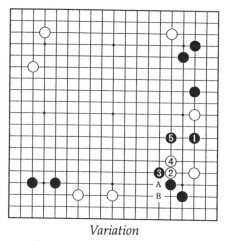

Variation

White could also attach with 2. Black will hane with 3, then jump to 5. The cut at A might look worrisome, but Black can secure his stones at the bottom by playing an atari at B. (See Problem 17 in *Get Strong at Invading*, Volume 5 in this series.)

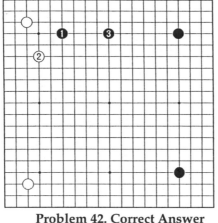

Problem 42. Correct Answer

A high large-knight's approach with 1 is the perfect move. White will most likely respond with 2, then Black will occupy the star point in the middle of the upper side with 3.

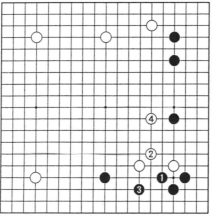

Problem 43. Correct Answer

Before anything else, Black must play 1, then take territory at the bottom with 3. After White caps at 4, this skirmish will come to a pause, but Black still has attacking chances.

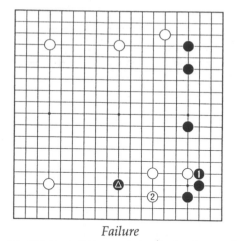

Failure

If Black crawls at 1, White will jump into the bottom with 2, separating the marked stone from its allies on the right. This stone could come under attack later on.

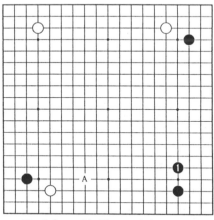

Problem 44. Correct Answer

Black should make a corner enclosure with 1 and aim to make a pincer at A.

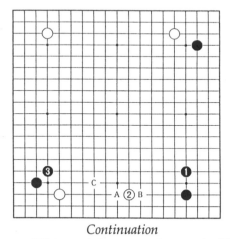

Continuation

White might next play at 2. (If White 2 at A, Black can make an ideal checking extension from his corner enclosure with B.) Black can now continue with either 3 or C.

Problem 45. Black to Play

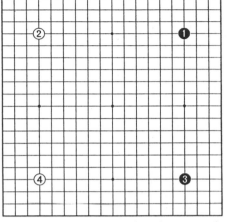

Both Black and White have made *niren-seis*. If Black wants to make an approach move on the left, where should he play?

Problem 46. Black to Play

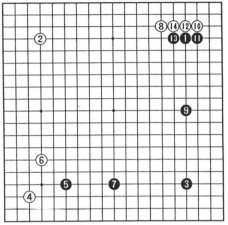

After White 14, how should Black play so as to make the most efficient use of his moyo below?

Problem 47. White to Play

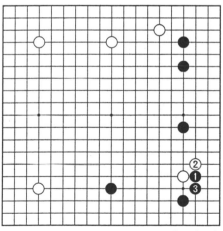

Black 1 violates the proverb which instructs us not to attach against weak stones. After Black draws back with 3, where should White play?

Problem 48. White to Play

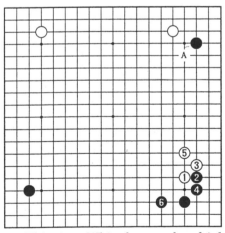

This time White has made a high approach with 1. Instead of the diagonal move at A, Black plays the joseki to 6. How should White continue?

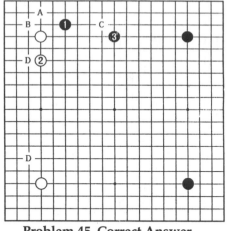

Problem 45. Correct Answer

Black 1 is the usual approach move. If White answers with 2, Black will extend to 3. In response to White 2, Black could also play the sequence Black A–White B–Black C. Approaching between White's *niren-sei* formation at one of the points D is rarely played.

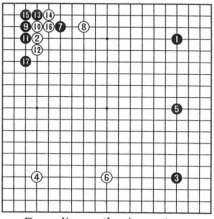

Depending on the circumstances

If Black had a *sanren-sei* formation on the right, the sequence in the correct answer might not be to White's liking because Black would have built up a large moyo. In that case, he would pincer with 8, making a thick position at the top with the sequence to 16.

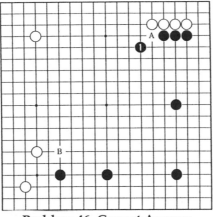

Problem 46. Correct Answer

Black 1 is the vital point of Black's moyo. Without this move, White would turn at A and the three black stones in the upper right would become heavy. Jumping to Black B instead of 1 is also a good move, but Black must take countermeasures against White A first.

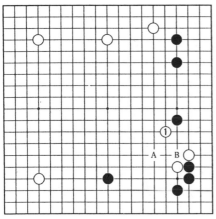

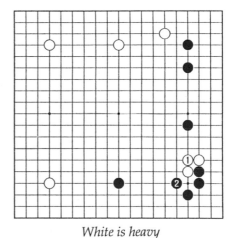

Problem 47. Correct Answer

When your opponent's stones are strong, you must play lightly to make *sabaki*. White 1 or White A is such a move. Cutting at B would be a bad move for Black.

White is heavy

Connecting at 1 leaves White with a heavy group. After Black 2, it becomes a good target to attack.

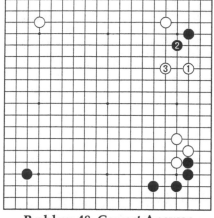

Problem 48. Correct Answer

White should pincer the black stone in the upper right corner with 1. If Black plays 2, White will jump to 3 and make a moyo on the right side. Black's stones are still under attack, so White will end in sente.

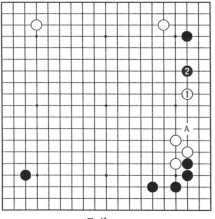

Failure

Playing the joseki move of White 1 is not good. Black can settle his stone in the upper right corner by extending to 2 and threaten to invade White's position at the bottom with a move at A. (See Problems 30, 33, 36, 39, and 42 in *Get Strong at Invading*.)

Problem 49. Black to Play

Problem 50. Black to Play

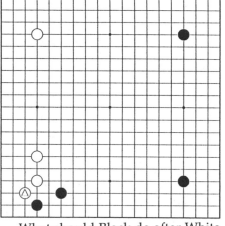

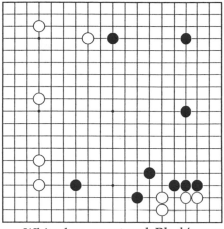

What should Black do after White plays the marked stone?

White has countered Black's *san-ren-sei* opening with a Chinese opening. Where should Black play?

Problem 51. Black to Play

Problem 52. White to Play

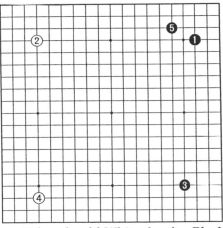

White 1 is a light move. You might think that the cutting point at A is a serious weakness in White's position, but Black must not cut there. What should he do instead?

What should White do after Black makes a corner enclosure with 5?

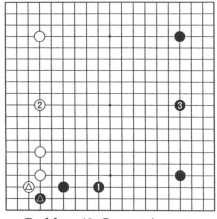

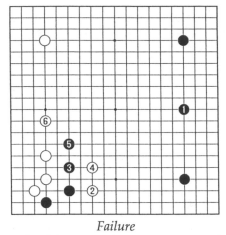

Problem 49. Correct Answer

After exchanging the marked stones, Black must extend to 1. White 2 would then be the usual move in this position and Black would make a *san-ren-sei* on the right side with 3.

Failure

Rushing to make a *sanren-sei* with 1 is bad. White 2 and 4 severely attack the black stones, robbing them of a base. After Black 5, White takes profit on the left side with 6.

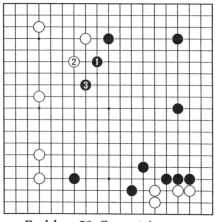

Problem 50. Correct Answer

Black 1 is the focal point of the two moyos. If White defends his moyo with 2, Black keeps advancing with 3, making the scale of his moyo even greater while diminishing the scale of White's.

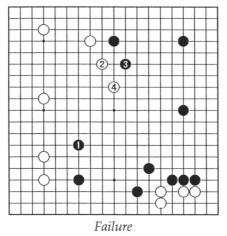

Failure

Black 1 is also a good point because it strengthens his thin position at the bottom. However, White takes the vital point of 2 and marches into Black's sphere of influence with 4.

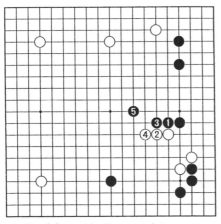

Problem 51. Correct Answer

Black 1 and 3 are the most natural moves. After White 4, Black jumps to 5 and a black moyo on the right side emerges. Moreover, White's stones are still not settled.

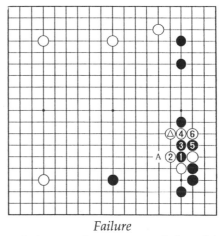

Failure

It is tempting to cut at 1, but this falls into a trap. White forces with the sequence to 6 and Black's potential territory and moyo on the upper right suddenly disappears.

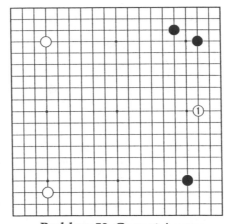

Problem 52. Correct Answer

White should break up Black's formation on the right side by playing at 1.

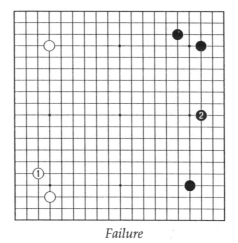

Failure

Making a corner enclosure in the lower left corner with 1 is passive. Black will take this opportunity to build a strong formation on the right side with 2, which is an ideal extension from both the corner enclosure at the top and the star point at the bottom.

Problem 53. Black to Play

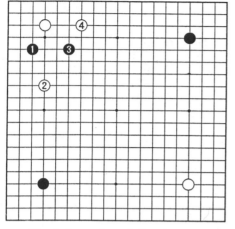

Black has played the two corner star points on diagonally opposite sides of the board. After the sequence from Black 1 to White 4, how should Black continue?

Problem 54. White to Play

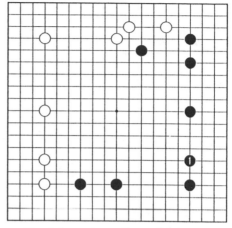

Black has strengthened his moyo on the right, but this is not a good move, as it is premature. Where should White play to punish Black for his mistake?

Problem 55. Black to Play

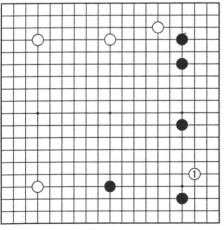

White 1 is a bad move. How should Black answer?

Problem 56. Black to Play

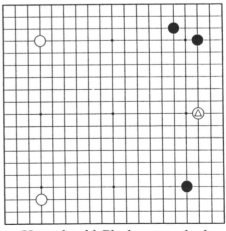

How should Black respond after White plays his marked stone?

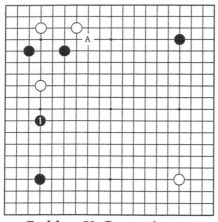

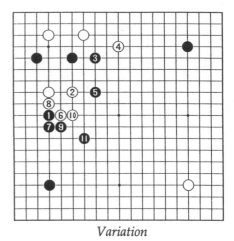

Problem 53. Correct Answer

Black should either make a pincer around 1 or press White at A.

Variation

A severe one-space pincer against the white stone is also frequently played in professional games. After White 2, Black forces with 3, then caps at 5. The sequence to Black 11 is one possible continuation.

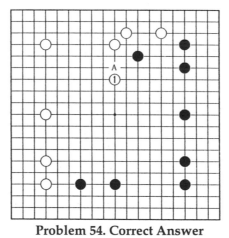

Problem 54. Correct Answer

White 1 (or A) is the focal point of the two opposing moyos. This move expands White's moyo while reducing the scale of Black's.

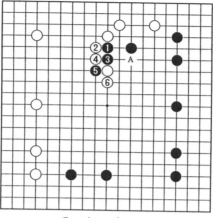

Continuation

The two-space jump of White 1 is thinner than the tight one-space jump at A in the correct answer, but it is a lot more severe. Don't worry about Black trying to break through with the sequence from 1 to 5. After 6, White can aim at A or capture the black stone at 5 in a ladder.

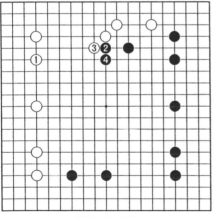

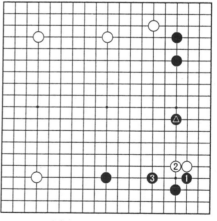

| *White's failure* | **Problem 55. Correct Answer** |

White misses his chance to seize the initiative when he meekly defends with 1. Black expands the scale of his moyo with 2 and 4. White has fallen behind.

Attaching with Black 1 is the only move. It robs White of his base and, when White stands at 2, Black launches a powerful attack on the two white stones with 3.

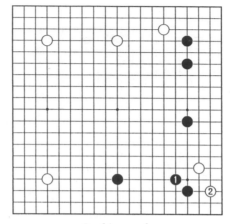

Lacking a plan

Black 1 is a lukewarm move. White is happy to slide to 2, making a base for his stones in the lower right.

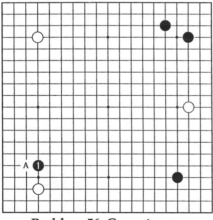

Problem 56. Correct answer

It is best for Black to make an approach move at 1 or A to prevent White from making a corner enclosure.

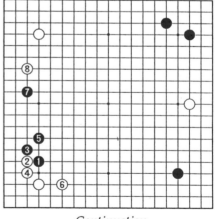

Continuation

If White attaches at 2, the joseki to Black 7 will follow. Attacking Black's formation on the left with White 8 is now the most reasonable move.

Problem 57. Black to Play

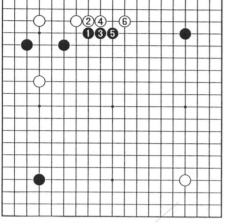

Black will sometimes press White at the top with the sequence to 5. What should Black do after White 6?

Problem 58. Black to Play

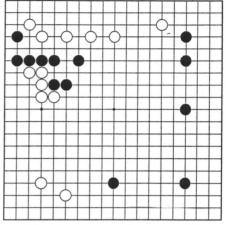

Black's stones in the upper left are a bit cramped. How should he play so as to take the lead in this game?

Problem 59. Black to Play

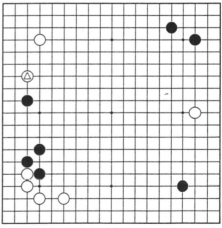

White has extended all the way to 1. How should Black respond?

Problem 60. Black to Play

The marked white stone threatens to invade the black formation on the left side. Should Black defend against this threat or is there something else he should do?

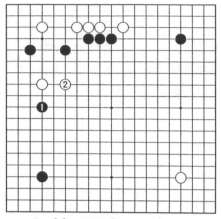

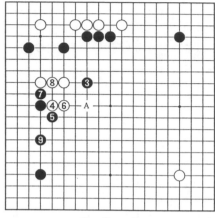

Problem 57. Correct Answer

Black must utilize his thickness along the top by pincering with 1. If White jumps to 2 —

Continuation

Black caps at 3. After the sequence to White 8, Black can play at 9 or A. For an analysis of the joseki in the problem diagram, refer to *Get Strong at Joseki 1*, Problems 142, 144, 148, 151, 156, and 158.

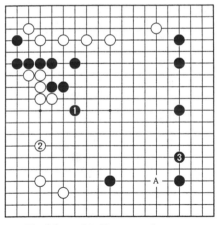

Problem 58. Correct Answer

Black should play the knight's move at 1. This move threatens the five white stones in the upper left side, so White must respond with 2. If White omits this move, Black 3 at 2 is a severe attack. Next, Black strengthens his moyo on the right with 3 (or A).

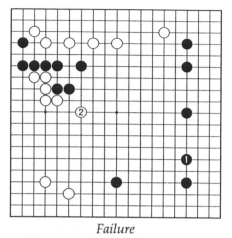

Failure

If Black immediately strengthens the right side with 1, White will take the initiative with the knight's move of 2, expanding his moyo on the left and attacking the black stones in the upper left. Moreover, the potential scale of Black's moyo has been greatly reduced.

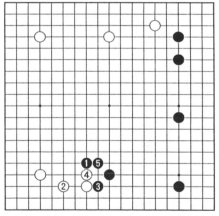

Problem 59. Correct Answer

Black should expand his moyo by capping with 1. This move is in keeping with the spirit of the Chinese opening. White 2 is the proper response, but Black thickens his position in the center by attaching at 3 and drawing back with 5.

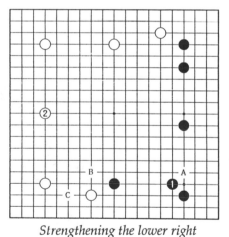

Strengthening the lower right

Making a corner enclosure with Black 1 or A is not necessarily bad, but it is a little bit slack. White can make an ideal moyo on the left with 2. If Black now caps at B, White has other responses besides C.

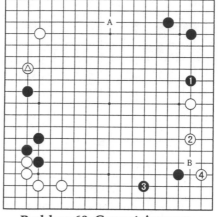

Problem 60. Correct Answer

Instead of defending against the marked stone, Black should start operations against the white stone on the right side by extending from his corner enclosure above with 1. The sequence to White 4 is the best continuation. If White 4 at A, Black B takes the corner territory while attacking the white stones above.

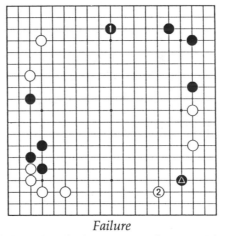

Failure

Black must not rush to play the big point at the top with 1. White would then take the initiative at the bottom by playing a double approach against the marked black stone with 2.

Problem 61. White to Play

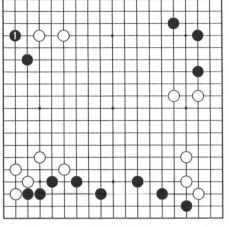

How should White respond to Black 1?

Problem 62. Black to Play

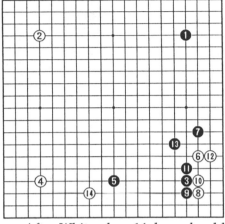

After White plays 14, how should Black respond?

Problem 63. Black to Play

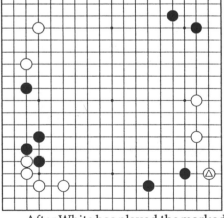

White concentrates on building his own moyo by making a *sanren-sei* with 1, ignoring what Black might do next. How should Black play?

Problem 64. Black to Play

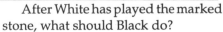

After White has played the marked stone, what should Black do?

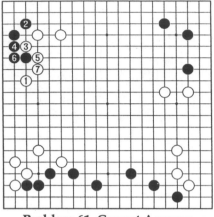

Problem 61. Correct Answer

Taking into account his position in the lower left, White should pincer with 1. With the sequence to 7, White gets a thick position in the center which works well with his stones on the lower left.

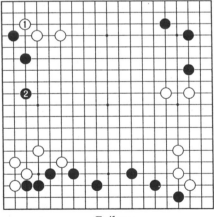

Failure

White 1 is a passive move. Black will take this opportunity to extend to 2, establishing a position on the left side while inhibiting the development of White's position below.

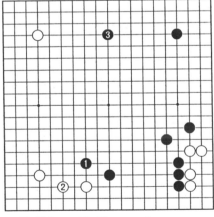

Problem 62. Correct Answer

Black should cap with 1. White will most likely respond with 2, so Black can take the big point at the top with 3, mapping out a magnificent sphere of influence.

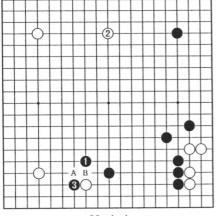

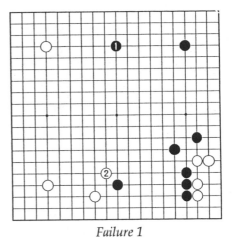

<table>
<tr><td>Variation</td><td>Failure 1</td></tr>
</table>

Variation

If White takes the big point at 2 and doesn't defend the bottom, the attachment of Black 3 is big. If White A, Black will cut at B and he will have no problem defending his position here.

Failure 1

If Black rushes to play 1, White expands his position with 2, while limiting the scale of Black's moyo.

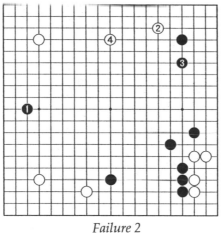

Failure 2

Trying to gain a foothold on the left side with 1 is dubious. White will establish a position at the top with 2 and 4. A move like 1 is played when Black intends to go for territory, so it is inconsistent with his moyo strategy here.

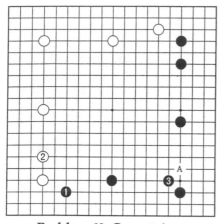

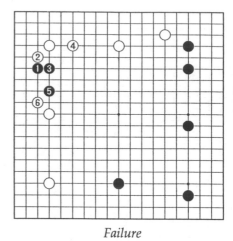

Problem 63. Correct Answer

Black should approach with 1, then, when White answers with 2, strengthen his corner with 3 or A. Black has taken the initiative and is on the road to victory.

Failure

In this kind of a position, Black must never make an approach move inside White's sphere of influence, for he will come under a severe attack with the sequence from 2 to 6.

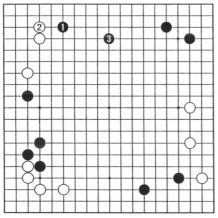

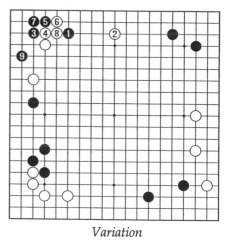

Problem 64. Correct Answer

Black should approach with 2. If White defends the corner with 2, Black will extend to 3, making a moyo in the upper right.

Variation

White might pincer the black stone at 1 with 2. In that case, Black would take the corner territory with the sequence from 3 to 9. Black should be satisfied with this result.

Problem 65. Black to Play

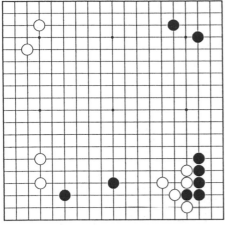

There are big points still to be played on the left side and at the top, but Black has an even bigger point somewhere else. Where should he play?

Problem 66. White to Play

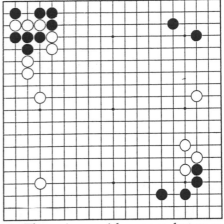

There is a wide space between White's thickness on the upper left and his stone below. However, Black has a good attacking move on the upper right. What should White do?

Problem 67. Black to Play

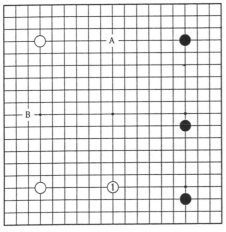

In this variation of the Chinese opening, White takes the star point in the middle of the lower side. How should Black respond?

Problem 68. Black to Play

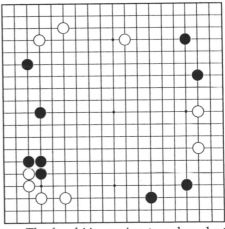

The fuseki is coming to a close, but there are still important points left. Where is Black's biggest move?

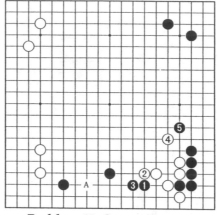

Problem 65. Correct Answer

Black 1 is a huge move. It attacks the white group on the right and defends against an invasion at A. After Black 5, White's group is still unstable and Black will build a moyo on the right side while attacking White.

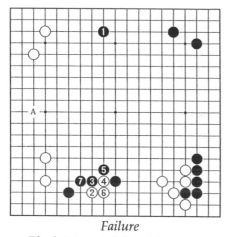

Failure

Black 1 is certainly a big point, as is Black A on the left side, but the invasion of White 2 and 4 is severe. With the sequence to 8, White has settled his stones at the bottom and disrupted Black's stones there.

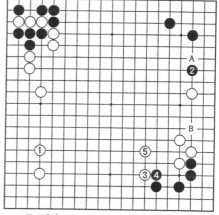

Problem 66. Correct Answer

White might be tempted to extend to A on the right side, but, in this case, it is better to strengthen the stone in the lower left with 1. If Black now plays 2, White will play 3 and 5, mapping out a large-scale moyo. Note that White 5 indirectly defends against the invasion at B.

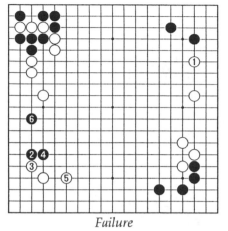

Failure

If White extends to 1, Black approaches at 2 and breaks up White's position on the left side with the sequence to 6. The effectiveness of White's thickness above is now neutralized.

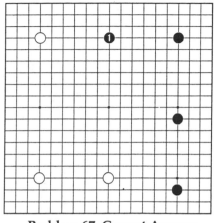

Problem 67. Correct Answer

Black should take the big point at 1 to map out a large-scale moyo in the upper right.

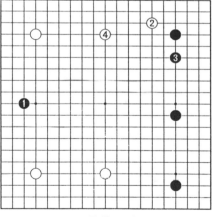

Failure 1

Jumping in between White's two star-point stones on the left side is not good. Black's natural strategy of making a large-scale moyo at the top is thwarted by White 2 and 4.

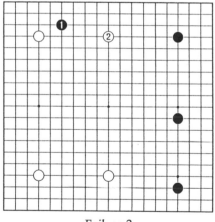

Failure 2

There are many examples in professional games of Black approaching with 1, but when he plays this way, White will pincer at 2 and Black can no longer play a moyo strategy.

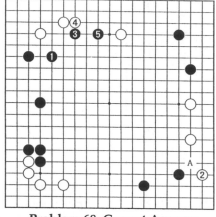

Problem 68. Correct Answer

Black 1 is the biggest move. If White were to play there, he would be able to build a moyo at the top. White 2 is necessary to prevent Black A, which defends the corner and attacks the white stones. However, Black will next wipe out White's potential territory at the top with 3 and 5.

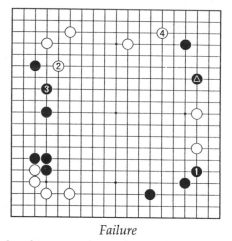

Failure

Black 1 is certainly a big point, but White will force with 2, building a moyo at the top, then approach with 4. Note that the marked black stone is two spaces away from the white formation below, so White's stones there are not being attacked all that severely.

Problem 69. Black to Play

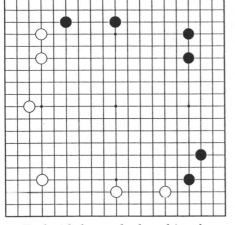

Each side has staked out his sphere of influence. However, Black must now invade White's moyo. Where should he play?

Problem 70. Black to Play

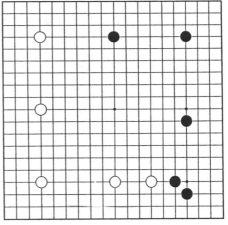

All the big points have been taken, with both sides staking out their own moyos. Where should Black play next?

Problem 71. White to Play

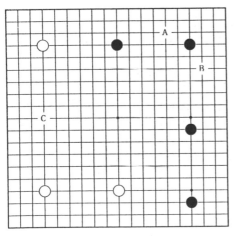

Where should White play in this position? Should he make an approach move at one of the points A or B, or should he map out a moyo at C?

Problem 72. White to Play

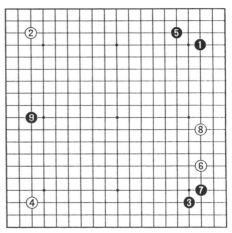

In this opening, all the corners have been occupied and Black has taken a big point with 9. Where should White play next?

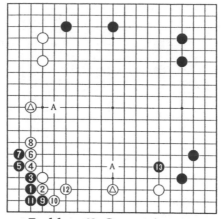

Problem 69. Correct Answer

Black should invade the lower left corner with 1. Since both the marked white stones are on the third line, White can't expect to make a large-scale moyo because Black can cap at one of the points marked A. If White blocks with 2 and plays the sequence to 12, Black will cap at 13 to build his own moyo on the right side and prevent White from making one himself.

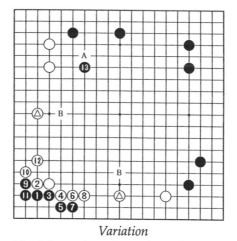

Variation

White could also block from the other side with 2. This time, however, Black will map out his moyo at the top with 13. This move also neutralizes White's thickness below. If Black omits this move, White will map out a large-scale moyo by playing at A. After 13, Black still has capping moves at the points B.

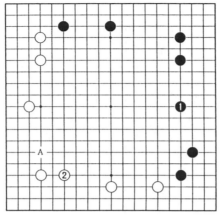

Failure

If Black continues to map out his own territory by taking the big point at 1, White will defend his position with 2 (or A) and Black will have a harder time erasing White's moyo. That is not to say that Black has a bad position, but, by not playing as in the correct answer, he has lost his chance to decisively take the lead.

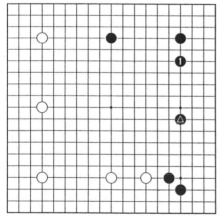

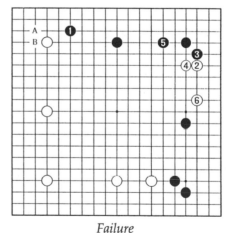

Problem 70. Correct Answer

Now is the time for Black to solidify his moyo. He should play 1 in the direction of the marked stone so as to strengthen the thinnest part of his position.

Failure

Expanding his moyo with 1 is certainly a good point, but White will approach at 2. With the sequence to White 6, Black's moyo has been erased. Black can aim at the invasion of A, but White would block at B and build a moyo along the left side.

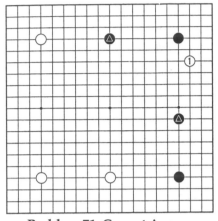

Problem 71. Correct Answer

White should approach with 1. The marked stone on the right is more widely spaced than the one at the top, so White has more room to expand.

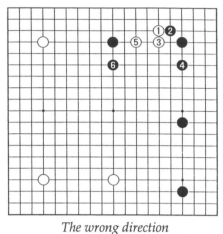

The wrong direction

White 1 is in the wrong direction. After 4, White has to play a narrow extension with 5. Black jumps out into the center with 6 and is satisfied.

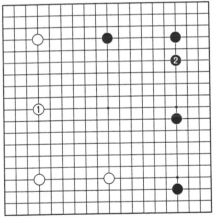

Failure

Making a *sanren-sei* on the left side with 1 is quite appealing, but 2 is too good a point to allow Black to take. With one move, Black solidifies his moyo in the top right.

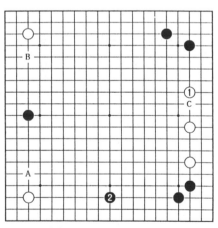

Problem 72. Correct Answer

White 1 is the only move. Black 2, Black A, or Black B all have the same value. If White plays 1 at 2, Black C would be a severe attack against the white stones. Black C is also an ideal extension from his corner enclosure above.

Problem 73. Black to Play

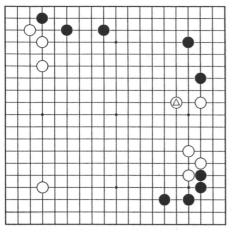

When White jumps into the center with the marked stone, the skirmish on the right side comes to a pause. Where should Black play next?

Problem 74. Black to Play

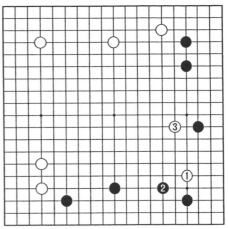

After 2, White strikes at the weak point of the low Chinese opening by capping at 3. How should Black prevent White from making *sabaki*?

Problem 75. Black to Play

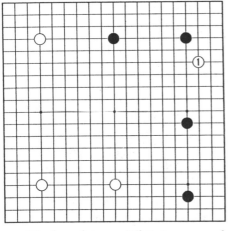

Black welcomes White's approach at 1. Now he can utilize the power of his Chinese-opening formation to attack White. Where is his strongest move?

Problem 76. White to Play

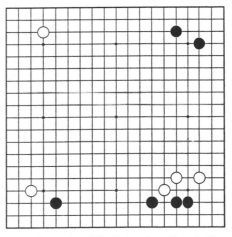

What should White do? Should he make a corner enclosure or should he take a big point?

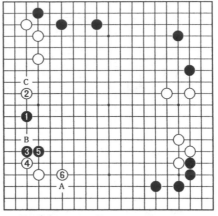

Problem 73. Correct Answer

Black should break up White's position on the left with 1. If White next plays 2, Black can extend to 3. After the exchange of White 4 for Black 5, White will play either 6 or A. If White 2 at B, Black will extend to C. No matter how White attacks, Black can easily settle his stones on the left side, so Black 1 is the perfect point to play.

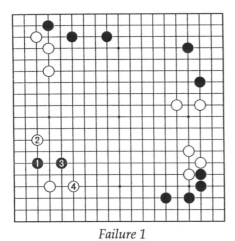

Failure 1

If Black plays an approach move with 1, White will pincer at 2. If Black jumps out to 3, White is satisfied by just jumping to 4.

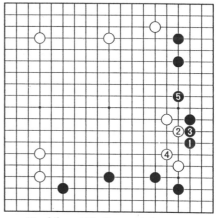

Problem 74. Correct Answer

Black 1 is a sharp move. White has to keep his stones linked, so he plays 2 and 4. When Black now plays 5, White's stones are left rootless, floating in the center, so Black will be able to gain more profit by attacking them.

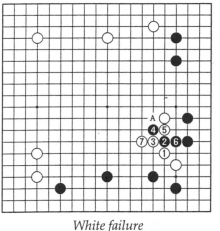

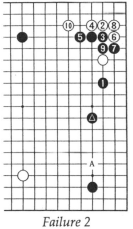

White failure

The forcing move of White 2 in the correct answer is necessary. If White simply plays 1, Black will play 2 and, after 7, Black can fight with A.

Black's failure

The proverb advises us to answer a cap with a knight's move, but if Black plays 1, White makes *sabaki* within Black's moyo, ending in sente.

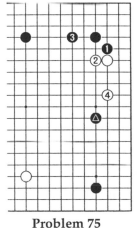

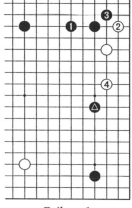

Problem 75
Correct Answer

Black should attach at 1, forcing White to stand at 2. Because of the marked stone, White can extend only as far as 4. Next, Black will attack the three white stones.

Failure 1

Black 1 is a bad move. White can settle his stones by sliding to 2 and extending to 4. As a result, the marked stone is misplaced and Black's Chinese-opening strategy has fallen apart.

Failure 2

The pincer of Black 1 is not good. White will invade with 2. After Black 10, the marked stone is too near the thickness above. This stone would be more efficient if it were at A.

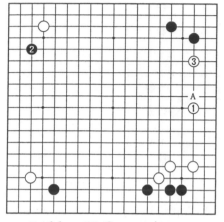

Problem 76. Correct Answer

Taking the big point of White 1 is the only move. White not only makes an extension from his three stones below, but he also limits how far Black can extend from his corner enclosure above. If Black makes an approach move at 2, White extends all the way to 3, threatening Black's corner enclosure. White 1 at A is also possible, but White 1 is the preferred move.

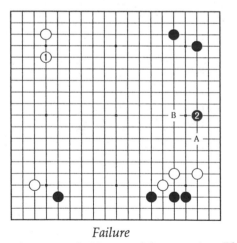

Failure

Making a corner enclosure with 1 is out of the question: Black 2 becomes too good a move. It is an ideal extension from his corner enclosure above and it makes the three white stones below thin. If White strengthens them by extending to A, Black jumps to B, expanding his moyo on the upper right side.

Problem 77. White to Play

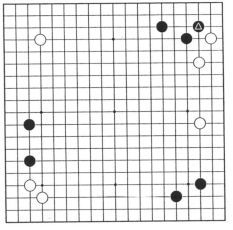

After Black defends the corner with the marked stone, where should White play?

Problem 78. White to Play

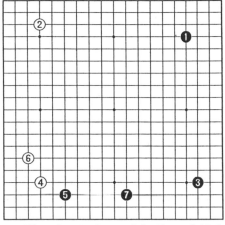

The formation of 3, 5, and 7 is known as the mini-Chinese opening. Where should White play next?

Problem 79. Black to Play

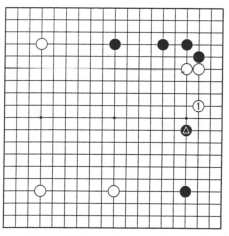

After White plays 1, the marked stone seems to be a bit thin. How should Black continue?

Problem 80. White to Play

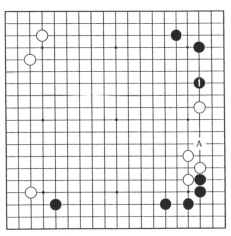

Black has just played 1, threatening to invade at A. How should White respond?

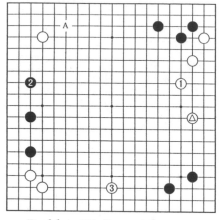

Problem 77. Correct Answer

The marked white stone is far away from its allies above, so White should defend at 1, which makes a good high-low balance. Black 2 is also a good move. Next, White extends along the bottom with 3, but White 3 at A would also be big.

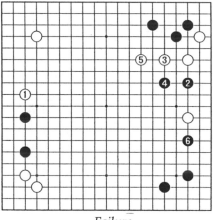

Failure

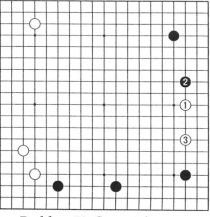

Problem 78. Correct Answer

White 1 is certainly a good attacking move, but Black will invade at 2. After the sequence to White 5, Black takes the initiative on the right side with the checking extension of 6.

If Black is able to take the big point (*oba*)on the right side, a large-scale moyo will come into being. Therefore, it is important for White to establish a presence there by playing 1. If Black 2, White settles his stones by extending to 3.

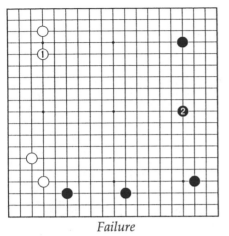

Failure

If White makes a corner enclosure with 1, Black will map out a large-scale moyo on the right side with 2. His opening strategy has been a great success.

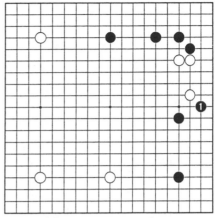

Problem 79. Correct Answer

Black should play 1, a move which attacks White and strengthens his position on the lower right.

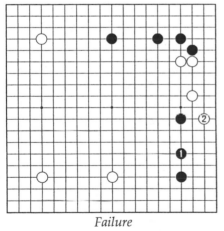

Failure

Making a corner enclosure with 1 is bad. White slides to 2, settling his stones while eating into Black's territory on the lower right side.

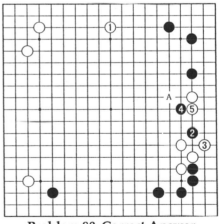

Problem 80. Correct Answer

Locally, White A is the proper move, but, taking the whole board into account, White should extend from his corner enclosure to 1. Even if Black invades at 2, White can fight and get a reasonable result.

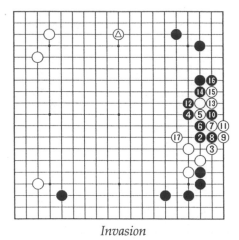

Invasion

For example, if Black invades at 2, then goes for thickness with the sequence from 4 to 16, White's group is safe and the marked white stone and 17 neutralize Black's thickness.

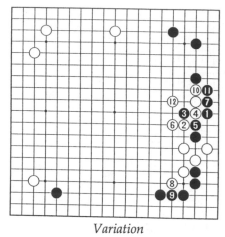

Variation

Instead of 4 in the previous diagram, Black could go for territory with 1 and 3 here. However, White settles his stones and gets thickness with the sequence to 12. (See *Get Strong at Invading*, Problems 27, 30, 33, 36, 39, and 42 for other variations of this joseki.)

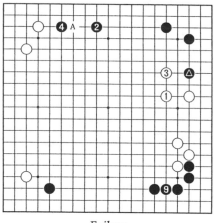

Failure

White 1 is the proper move, but this makes the marked stone a forcing move and Black can take the big point of 2. If White 3, Black extends to 4. If White plays 3 at A, Black will jump to 3.

Problem 81. Black to Play

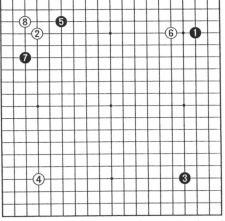

Against the double approach of Black 5 and 7, White anchors his stones in the corner with 8. What should Black do next?

Problem 82. Black to Play

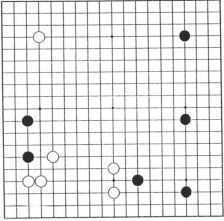

Black has played the Chinese opening on the right side. What should Black do in this position? Play for territory or make a moyo?

Problem 83. Black to Play

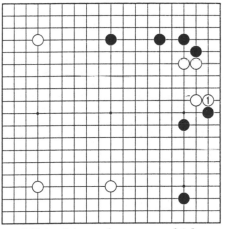

White 1 is a calm move which emphasizes the security of his stones. How should Black continue?

Problem 84. White to Play

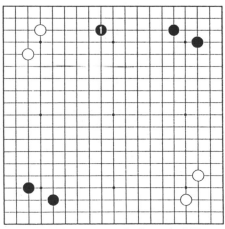

Black has extended to 1. Where should White play so as to maintain the balance of territories?

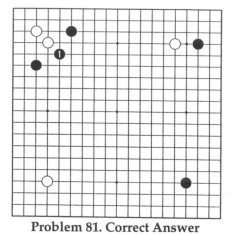

Problem 81. Correct Answer

Black should confine White to the corner with 1. Never hesistate to make such confining moves because they will give you a strategic advantage.

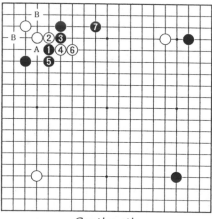

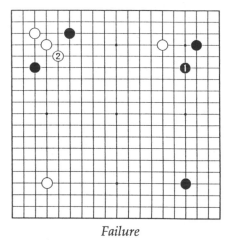

Continuation

When Black plays 1, he must expect White to cut through with 2 and 4. (Note that White could also play 2 from the other side at A.) In answer to White 6, Black will extend to 7. Black is now strong on the outside and he can also harass the white stones in the corner by playing on one of the points marked B.

Failure

Locally, Black 1 is a good move, but White takes command of the situation when he moves out into the center with 2. Black's two stones on the left can no longer play a part in a cohesive strategy.

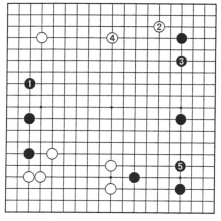

Problem 82. Correct Answer

When you play a stone on the star point, it is, in principle, important to develop influence and make a moyo, but there are times when it is more important to strengthen stones elsewhere, as in this position. Black should extend to 1. If White 2 and 4, Black takes territory with 3 and 5. All of Black's stones are now strong and he is ahead in territory.

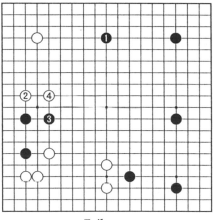

Failure

Black 1 is an excellent point with respect to his stones on the right side, but Black finds himself on the run when White attacks with 2 and 4.

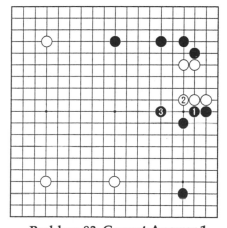

Problem 83. Correct Answer 1

Black should keep up the pressure on White by playing 1. If White 2, Black continues the attack with 3, a move which also expands Black's influence in the lower right.

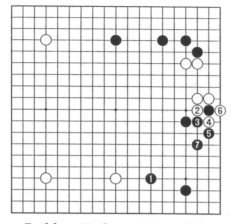

Problem 83. Correct Answer 2

Black could also extend to 1. If White secures his group with the sequence to 6, Black can connect with 7. He is satisfied with his profit in the lower right.

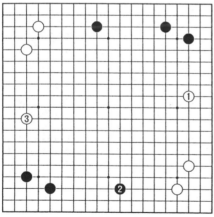

Problem 84. Correct Answer

It is imperative that White extend along the right side with 1. The remaining big points at 2 and 3 will now be shared by Black and White.

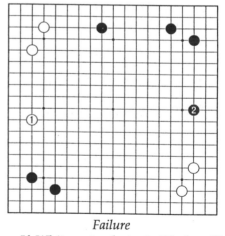

Failure

If White extends to 1, Black will make a double-wing formation from his corner enclosure in the upper right with 2. This is considered to be advantageous for Black.

Problem 85. Black to play

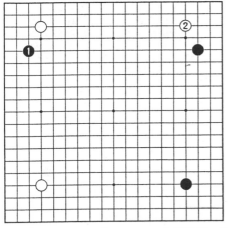

An approach move at White 2 would seem to be common sense to prevent Black from making a corner enclosure. But White 2 is a mistake. How should Black punish White?

Problem 86. Black to Play

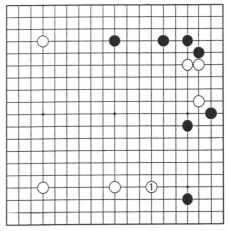

Suppose White doesn't defend his stones in the upper right and extends to 1 at the bottom instead. How should Black continue?

Problem 87. Black to Play

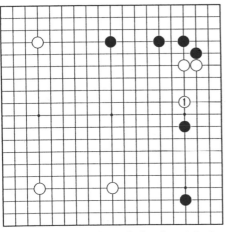

This time White defends with the extension of 1 on the fourth line. How should Black respond?

Problem 88. Black to Play

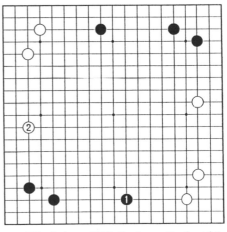

Black 1 and White 2 are the last big points (*oba*) of the fuseki. Where should Black play next?

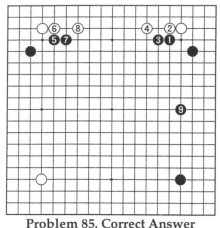

Problem 85. Correct Answer

Black should press White with 1 and 3, followed by 5 and 7. He then extends along the right side with 9.

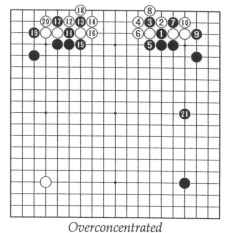

Overconcentrated

Black could also force White's stones at the top to become overconcentrated with the forcing sequence from 1 to 19. Black now has a big lead.

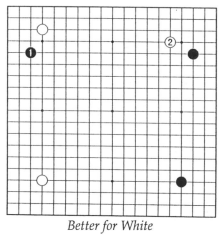

Better for White

If White wants to make an approach move, the high approach at 2 would give him a better result.

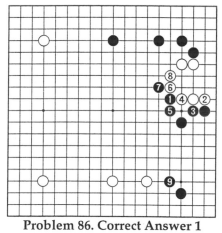

Problem 86. Correct Answer 1

The cap of Black 1 keeps up the pressure on White. After White 8, Black can defend his territory in the lower right with 9.

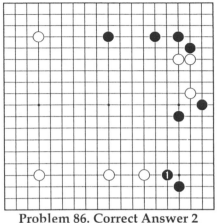

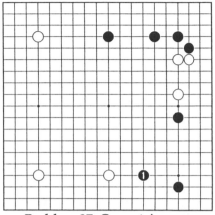

Problem 86. Correct Answer 2

It is also possible for Black to simply defend with the diagonal move of 1 and wait to see how White will play at the top.

Problem 87. Correct Answer

Black 1 is a flexible move. It defends against a white approach move.

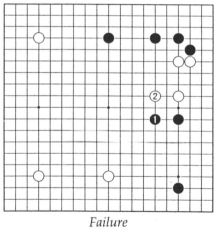

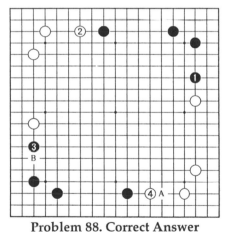

Failure

If Black jumps to 1, White will also jump out with 2. It is better for Black to defer this defense until later because, since White's stone on the upper right is high, he has no good way to invade on the side.

Problem 88. Correct Answer

The two-space extension of Black 1 is the biggest move. White will respond with 2. Next, Black 3 and White 4 are the natural continuation. However, Black 3 at A, followed by White 4 at B, is also possible. From here the middle game commences.

Problem 89. White to Play

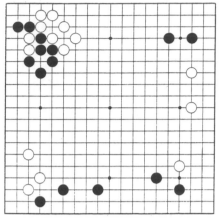

The proverb advises us, "Don't play near thickness!" White has thickness in the top left and Black on the upper left side, but White is thin on the right. Where should White play?

Problem 90. Black to play

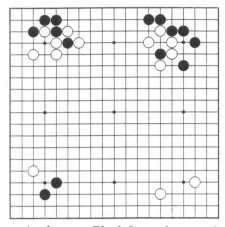

At the top, Black has taken profit while White has gotten influence in the center. Taking the whole board into consideration, where is Black's best move?

Problem 91. Black to Play

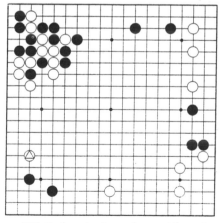

White has just made a wide extension from his thickness above with the marked stone. Where should Black play next?

Problem 92. Black to Play

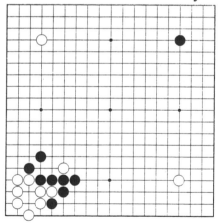

In the lower left corner, White has taken profit while Black has made thickness and ended in sente. Black must now make an approach move against one of the white stones. Which approach move should he make?

Problem 93. Black to Play

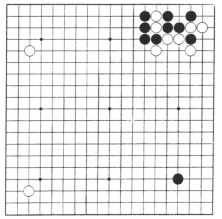

Black has made a thick position in the top right. He must now prevent White from making a corner enclosure in the upper left. How should Black approach the white stone there.

Problem 94. White to Play

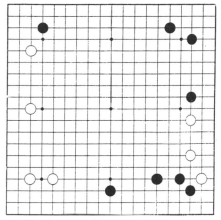

Playing at the top is now urgent, but whatever move White makes should have a relationship with his stones on the left side. Where should he play?

Problem 95. White to Play

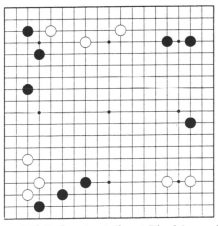

White has to strike at Black's weak point. If White doesn't play on this point, he will miss his chance to take the lead.

Problem 96. White to Play

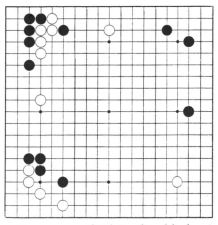

It seems as if White should play in the lower right or at the top. But look at the whole board before deciding on your move.

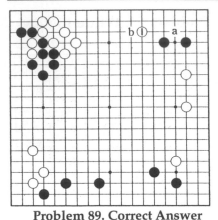

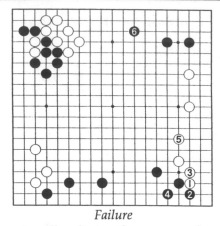

Problem 89. Correct Answer

White should extend all the way to 1. This move is the proper distance from his thickness on the left and it also aims at 'a', the weak point of Black's corner enclosure. White 1 at 'b' would be too close to his thickness.

Failure

Locally, playing the sequence from White 1 to 5 is good, but Black will then play 6, erasing the influence of White's thickness and defending the weak underbelly of his corner enclosure at the top.

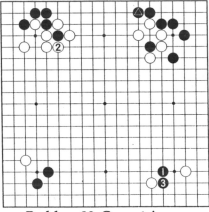

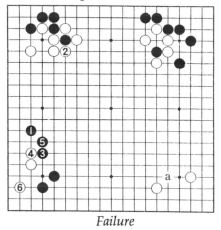

Problem 90. Correct Answer

Black should play 1, breaking the ladder. White has to capture with 2, so Black can then play 3, breaking through White's corner enclosure. Of course, White becomes thick when he captures, but the marked black stone serves to diminish the effect of this thickness.

Failure

Locally, the pincer of Black 1 is a good point, but White will capture with 2 and the *aji* of the ladder-breaking move disappears. Although Black will become thick with 3 and 5, White is also thick at the top, so it balances out. Moreover, White can live in the corner with 4 and 6.

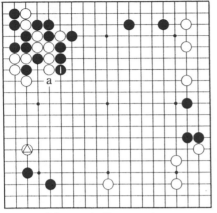

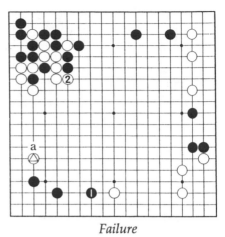

Problem 91. Correct Answer

Black 1 is a strong move because it expands Black's moyo at the top and threatens to force at 'a'. Instead of playing the marked stone, White could have turned at 1.

Failure

Responding to the marked stone by extending to 1 is not good. White turns at 2. If White played the marked stone at 2, Black would extend to 'a', neutralizing White's thickness above.

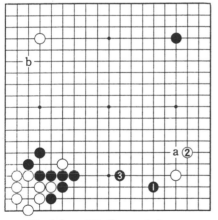

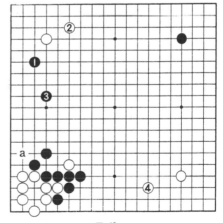

Problem 92. Correct Answer

Approaching the lower right corner with Black 1 is the best move. Black gets an ideal position at the bottom when he plays 3. Instead of 2, White 'a' is also a good move. An approach move at Black 'b' would be in the wrong direction.

Failure

If Black approaches the stone in the upper left with 1, Black cannot be certain of getting the territory on the left side after 3 because White has a big endgame move at 'a'. Next, White extends to 4, curtailing the influence of Black's thickness at the bottom.

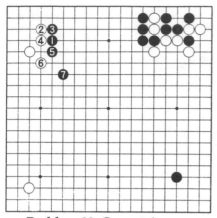

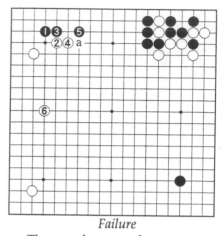

Problem 93. Correct Answer

The high approach of Black 1 works best with Black's thick position in the upper right. Even though White gets territory in the corner, Black maps out a moyo at the top with the sequence to 7.

Failure

The usual approach move at 1 is not good. White presses Black into a low position with 2 and 4. After 5, White can map out a moyo on the left side with 6 or he can continue to press the black stones with 'a'.

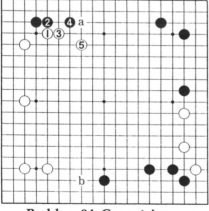

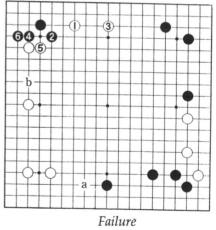

Problem 94. Correct Answer

White should press with 1 and 3, then jump to 5, mapping out a moyo on the left side. If Black next defends at 'a', White will fortify his position at the bottom by extending to 'b'. However, if White plays 1 at 'b', Black will play at 1 without hesitation.

Failure

If White pincers with 1, Black plays 2 to 6, securing the corner. If White now extends to 'a', Black invades at 'b', so White won't be able to make a moyo on the left side. If it were Black's turn, he would play 2, so White 1 provokes the move Black wants to play.

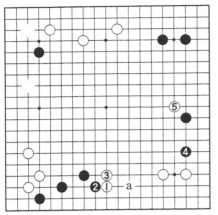

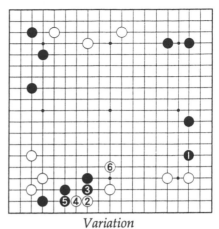

Problem 95. Correct Answer

Variation

White must play the checking extension of 1, attacking the weak underbelly of the three black stones and defending his own weak stones on the right. Black must play 2 and the sequence to 5 follows. If White omitted 1, Black would play at 'a'.

Black may not like the exchange of 2 for 3 in the correct answer because it strengthens White, but if he omits it, White will slide to 2. Black's stones are left without a base after White jumps to 6.

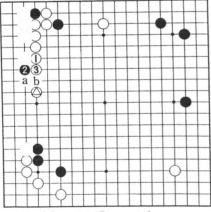

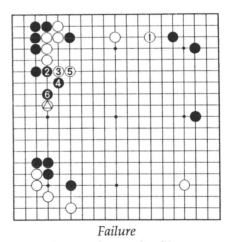

Problem 96. Correct Answer

Failure

It is essential that White maintain a link with the marked stone by pushing with 1 and 3. (If Black 'a' next, White 'b'.) These moves have increased Black's profit on the right, but White has become thick in compensation.

If White makes a checking extension with 1, Black will push up with 2 and 4, and, after Black 6, the marked white stone has become isolated and a black moyo on the left side comes into being.

Problem 97. White to Play

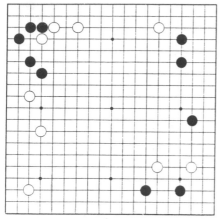

White's stones at the top are thin and it is clear that he must reinforce them. But choosing the right point is crucial. Where should White play?

Problem 98. Black to Play

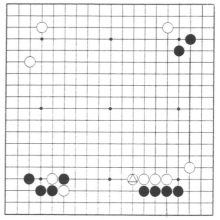

White has just extended with his marked stone, making a thick wall at the bottom. How should Black answer this move?

Problem 99. Black to Play

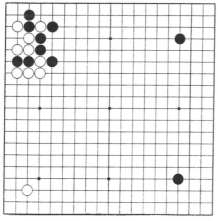

A joseki has been played out in the upper left corner and White has gotten a thick position on the upper left side. However, Black has kept sente. Where should he now play?

Problem 100. White to Play

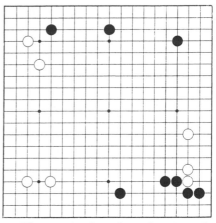

There are a lot of good points that White wants to play. However, one of these points takes precedence over all the others. Where should White play?

Problem 101. White to Play

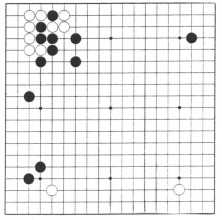

The joseki in the upper left corner has come to a pause. White has taken profit, but Black has thickness in the center. What should White do next?

Problem 102. White to Play

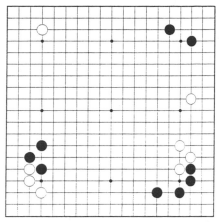

A basic joseki is in progress in the lower left corner. Should White complete the joseki or is there something else he should do?

Problem 103. Black to Play

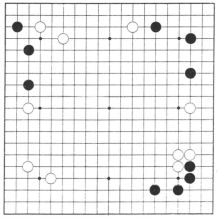

Black and White have established positions in all four corners and on the sides. All of Black's positions are strong, so Black should now go on the offensive. Where should he play?

Problem 104. Black to Play

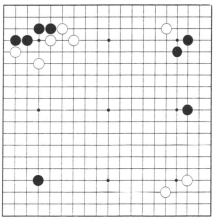

Even though only one stone has been played in the lower left corner, there is no hurry for Black to play in this part of the board; the upper right takes precedence. Where should Black play?

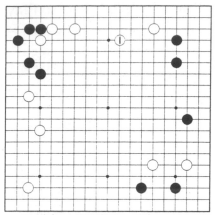

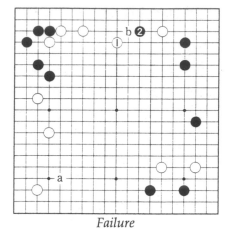

Problem 97. Correct Answer

White 1 is the perfect point: not too far from his stone on the right and an ideal distance from his three stones on the left. Playing this move high on the fourth line also strikes a good balance with his stones on the third line.

Failure

You may not think that one line to the right makes much of a difference, but, if White plays 1 here, his position at the top right is still thin and Black will invade with 2. If White plays 1 at 'a', Black will invade at 'b'.

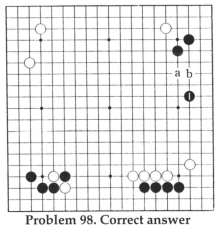

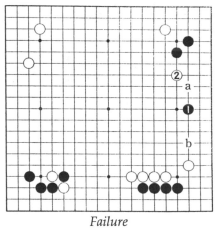

Problem 98. Correct answer

Black must extend down the right side to neutralize White's thickness, but because White is so thick below Black should extend only as far as 1. Next, if White 'a', Black can defend at 'b'; if White 'b', Black 'a'.

Failure

Extending one line farther with 1 leaves Black vulnerable to an invasion at 2 or 'a'. White may not make this invasion immediately, but Black must always worry about it. Black could settle his stone with 'b', but White will use his thickness below to attack.

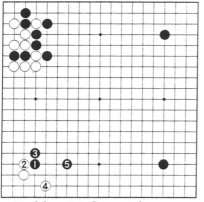

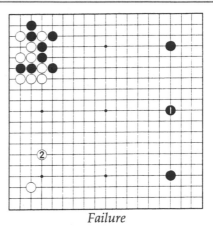

Problem 99. Correct Answer

Since White's stone in the lower left corner is low, Black can strike at 1. The reason that Black chose the joseki in the upper left was because he had this move. Crawling with 2 is the right direction. After Black 5, White's thickness has been neutralized.

Failure

It is not appropriate for Black to make a *sanren-sei* in this position. White will extend to 2, making an ideal position on the left side. If Black wanted to make a *sanren-sei*, he should have played differently in the upper left corner.

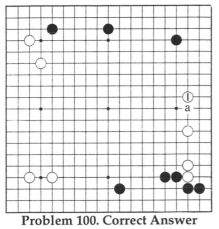

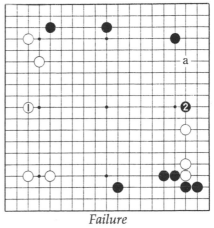

Problem 100. Correct Answer

The extension of White 1 is the most important point on the board for White. With this move, all of his groups are strong. If Black is allowed to make a checking extension to 'a', the game could become difficult for White.

Failure

White gets a nice position on the left if he plays 1, but the checking extension of Black 2 leaves the white stones vulnerable and White must defend them. But Black will make profit by attacking them. If White 1 at 'a', Black 2 is still a severe move.

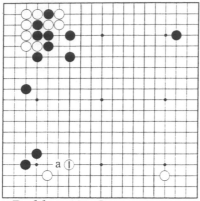

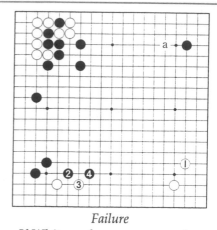

Problem 101. Correct Answer

Although it is important to quickly make an approach move or a corner enclosure in the fuseki, White 1 is an urgent move that must be played before any other. It is played to counter Black's thickness at the top left and to prevent him from pressing at 'a'.

Failure

If White makes a corner enclosure at 1 or an approach move at 'a', Black will immediately play 2 and 4, and an enormous moyo comes into being on the left. The moves to Black 4 are a joseki. (See Problem 49 in *Get Strong at Joseki 1*.)

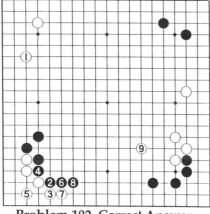

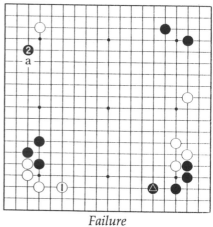

Problem 102. Correct Answer

White should make a corner enclosure with 1 and let Black attach with 2. White will secure his stones in the lower left corner with the sequence to 7. Black makes a thick position on the outside with 8, but this thickness is neutralized when White jumps to 9.

Failure

With the marked black stone in place, playing the joseki with White 1 is not very efficient. Black can now seize the initiative on the left side with an approach move at 2 or 'a'. You should never blindly follow a joseki without looking at the whole board.

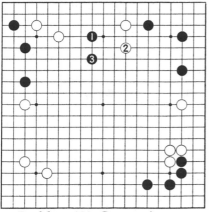

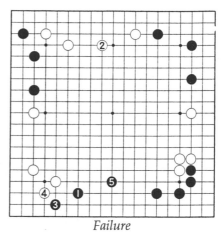

Problem 103. Correct Answer

Since White's position at the top is thin and Black has strong positions on the left and the right, Black should seize the initiative by invading at 1. After the exchange of 2 for 3, White is left with weak stones on the left and on the right. Black has taken the lead.

Failure

The checking extension of Black 1 is certainly a good move, but with respect to the whole board, it is not the focal point of the game. White will defend the top with 2 and Black has lost his chance to take the decisive lead as in the correct answer diagram.

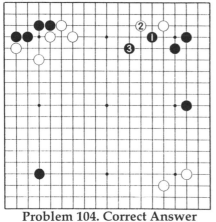

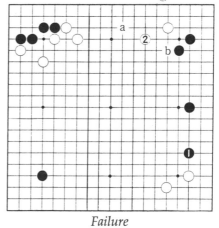

Problem 104. Correct Answer

It is important for Black to inhibit White's expansion in the upper right with 1 and 3. With these moves, a black moyo emerges and White is prevented from making one for himself.

Failure

The checking extension of Black 1 is a big move, but White will play 2, making it hard for Black to take measures against White at the top. Black 1 at 'a' is greedy: White would take the initiative by attaching at 'b'.

Problem 105. Black to Play

Problem 106. Black to Play

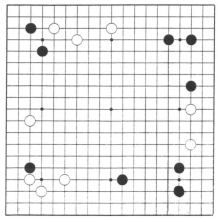

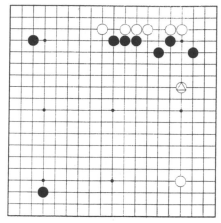

There are a number of big extensions that Black can play. Which one is the biggest?

The marked white stone is in the shadow of Black's thick wall at the top. How should Black attack it?

Problem 107. White to Play

Problem 108. Black to Play

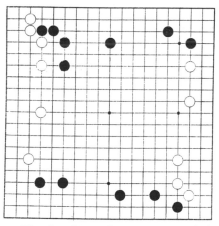

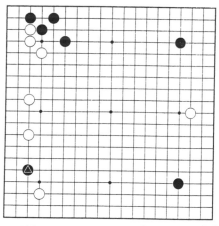

The fuseki is almost over and the middle game is about to begin. Where should White play?

White is strong on the upper left side, so what should Black do about his marked stone in the lower left?

Problem 109. Black to Play

Problem 110. Black to Play

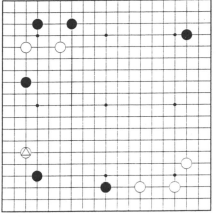

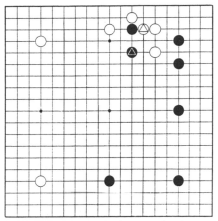

The marked white stone on the left is outnumbered. How should Black attack it?

In answer to Black's marked stone, White has strengthened his position at the top with his own marked stone. How should Black continue?

Problem 111. Black to Play

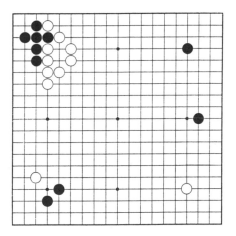

White has a very thick position at the top left. Black wants to counter this thickness. What is the best move for him to do this?

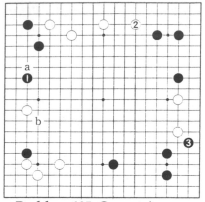

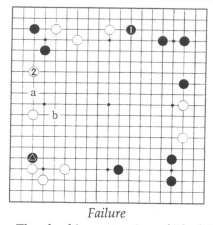

Problem 105. Correct Answer

If White makes a checking extension at 'a', the two black stones in the upper left will come under a strong attack. Therefore, Black extends to 1 to prevent this. The reason Black extends tightly to 1 is because he intends to make a shoulder hit at 'b' next. White 2 and Black 3 are the normal continuation.

Failure

The checking extension of Black 1 is also a good move, but White 2 is too big to allow; the two black stones there could find themselves uprooted and they would have to run for their lives. Black 1 at 'a' would provoke White to jump to 'b' and the marked black stone would be swallowed up in the white moyo. After this, White could aim at the invasion of 2.

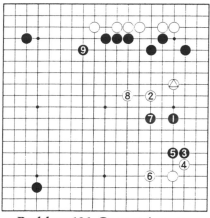

Problem 106. Correct Answer

Black doesn't want to pincer too severely because White might decide to sacrifice his marked stone. Thefore, Black plays a two-space pincer with 1. If White plays 2, Black approaches with 3. With the sequence to 9, Black is making good use of his thickness at the top.

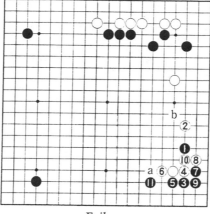

Failure

When Black plays the approach move of 1, he thinks that White is going to respond with 'a', enabling him to pincer the white stone by extending to 'b'. But this is too much to expect. White would pincer with 2 instead, and Black has no other alternative but to invade at 3. With the joseki to 11, White has made thickness at the bottom, effectively neutralizing Black's wall at the top.

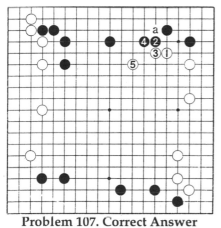

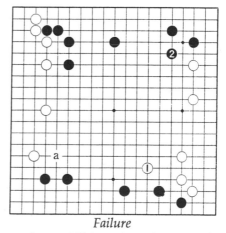

Problem 107. Correct Answer

White 1 is the vital point. When White plays here, he is expanding his own moyo on the right and preventing Black from expanding his moyo at the top. If Black doesn't answer White 1 and plays elsewhere, White will attach at 'a'.

Failure

Playing White 1 (or 'a') misses the point. Black will jump to 2 and a territorial moyo emerges at the top. If you compare this diagram with the correct-answer diagram, the difference should be obvious.

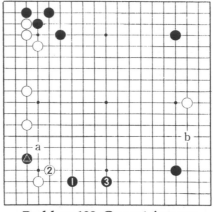

Problem 108. Correct Answer

Black should make a counterpincer with 1. When White makes the diagonal move of 2, Black can extend to 3, taking up a position at the bottom. By treating the marked stone lightly, Black puts the burden of what to do about this stone on White. If White next plays 'a', Black will extend to 'b'.

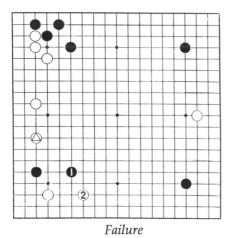

Failure

Against the two-space pincer of the marked white stone, Black 1 is the usual move, but White is strong on the left side, so White will just extend to 2, making territory while keeping up the pressure on Black.

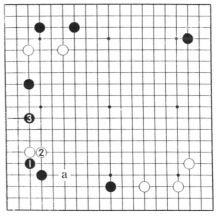

Problem 109. Correct Answer

Black should make a diagonal attachment with 1. White will stand at 2, but instead of jumping to 'a', Black will pincer with 3. The two white stones are now heavy and under attack.

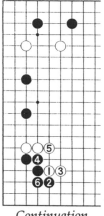

Continuation

If White attaches at 1, after the exchange of Black 2 for White 3, Black 4 is the vital point. After White 5, Black secures his stones in the corner with 6.

Failure

If Black jumps to 1, White plays the checking extension of 2, so Black's marked stone comes under attack.

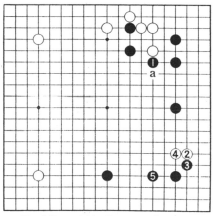

Problem 110. Correct Answer

Attaching with 1 is absolutely essential so that Black can maintain a connection with his two stones on the right. This move also maps out a vast moyo on the right side, so White must invade on the lower right with 2. However, Black goes on the attack with 3 and 5. If Black omits 1, White will jump to 'a'.

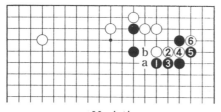

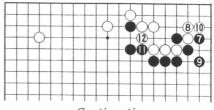

Variation

White might respond to Black 1 with the sequence to 6. He might also play 2 at 'a'. In that case, Black will cut at 'b', getting the advantage in the fight that follows.

Continuation

After White 6 in the previous diagram, Black sacrifices a stone when he ataris at 7 and ends in sente with the sequence to White 12.

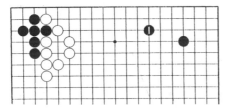

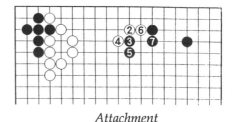

Problem 111. Correct Answer

The large knight's move of Black 1 is the ideal extension. It does not approach White's thickness too closely, yet it does not allow White to make a full extension from it.

Attachment

White 2 is as far as White can extend, but Black will attach with 3. White's stones at 2, 4, and 6 do not fully utilize his thickness, so they are not working efficiently.

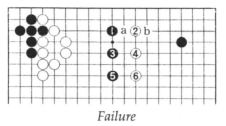

Failure

Black 1 is too near White's thickness. White will take the initiative by invading at 2. White now gets influence facing the right with the stones at 2, 4, and 6. If Black 1 at 'a', White will invade at 'b'.

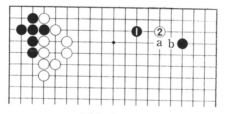

A bit dangerous

Black 1 is also a bit thin because White can invade at 2. If Black next attaches at 'a', White 'b' is a good counterattack.

Problem 112. Black to Play

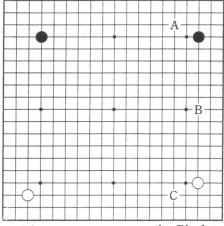

There are many ways for Black to play in this fuseki, but, if you were going to play on the right side, which one of the three moves from A to C would you choose?

Problem 113. Black to Play

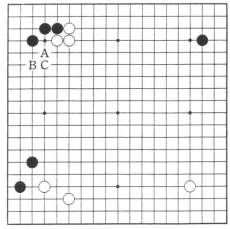

In the upper left corner, all the moves from A to C are josekis, but, in relation to Black's other stones, only one of these choices is correct. Which one is it?

Problem 114. White to Play

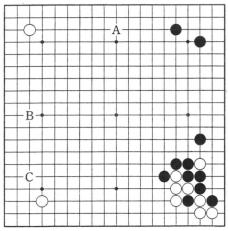

In the joseki played in the lower right, White ended in sente. Of the three moves indicated, which one would you choose for White?

Problem 115. Black to Play

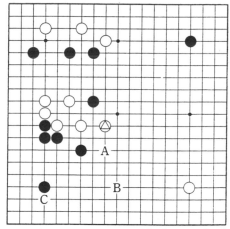

White runs away with the marked stone. Should Black continue attacking with A, map out a moyo with B or secure territory with C?

Problem 116. Black to Play

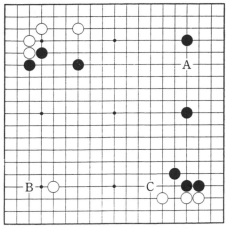

Black has played lightly in the upper left, so his stones there should encounter no problems and he can leave them as they are. Which of the three points indicated would you play?

Problem 117. Black to Play

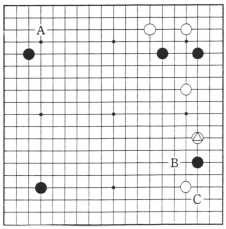

White has just pincered with the marked stone. Should White answer it by jumping to B, invading at C or making a corner enclosure with A?

Problem 118. Black to Play

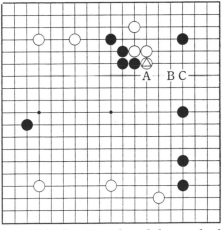

White has just played the marked stone in order to prevent Black from confining him to the top. How should Black respond: at A, B, or C?

Problem 119. Black to Play

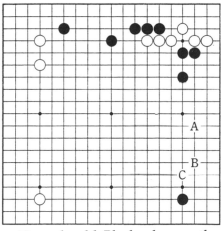

How should Black play on the right side: at A, B, or C?

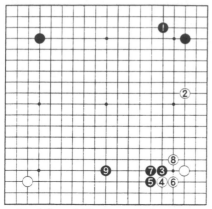

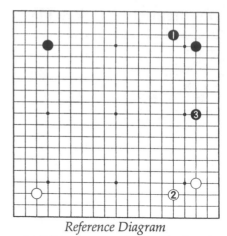

Problem 112. Correct Answer

Making a corner enclosure with 1 is the simplest way for Black to keep his first-move advantage. If Black 1 at 4, White can equalize by approaching at 1. White must extend to 2 to stop Black from making a moyo on the right, but Black takes up a position at the bottom with the joseki to 9.

Reference Diagram

If White responds to Black 1 by making a corner enclosure of his own with 2, Black will make an ideal extension with 3, taking control of the right side.

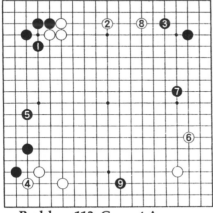

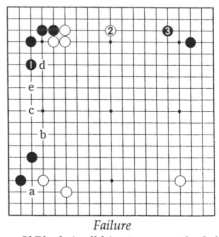

Problem 113. Correct Answer

The diagonal move of Black 1 is best. The sequence to Black 9 is one possible continuation. Black 5 and his stone at 1 now make an ideal high-low balance on the left side.

Failure

If Black 1, all his stones on the left are low. If White 'a' next, Black plays 'b' to maintain a high-low balance, but then an invasion at 'c' remains. If Black 1 at 'd', White 'e' is a severe attack.

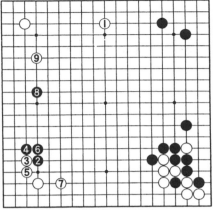

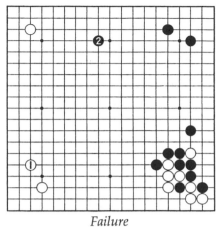

Problem 114. Correct Answer

Extending to 1 at the top is the right direction for White to play. This move will make it hard for Black to complete his moyo on the right side.

Failure

Making a corner enclosure with 1 on the left is not good. Black will be able to expand the scale of his moyo with 2, giving him the advantage.

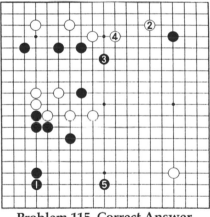

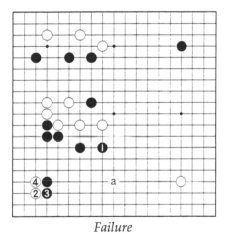

Problem 115. Correct Answer

The first thing that Black must do is to defend his territory on the left by enclosing the corner with 1. If White next approaches with 2, Black exchanges 3 for 4, then maps out a moyo with 5. If White 2 at 5, Black will play at the top.

Failure

Black 1 is not a very forceful attack. White will snatch the corner territory from Black with the 3–3 point invasion of 2. Against Black 1 at 'a', White will also invade at 2.

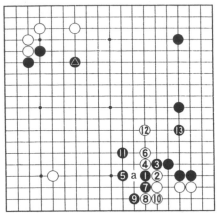

Problem 116. Correct Answer

Black 1 is the vital point. White cuts through with 2 and 4, and the joseki to 13 follows. The marked stone will have an influence on the ensuing fight. If White crawls to 7 with 2, Black will extend to 'a' and make a moyo in the center.

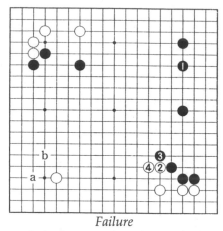

Failure

If Black strengthens his position in the upper right with 1, White will play 2 and 4, reducing the scale of Black's moyo on the right. If Black now approaches at 'a', White gets the advantage when he plays 'b'.

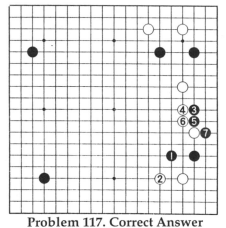

Problem 117. Correct Answer

Jumping to Black 1 is the ideal move. When White answers with 2, Black can invade with 3. After 7, Black's stones on the right side have a secure base.

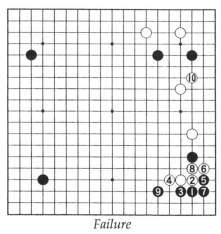

Failure

Invading with Black 1 is not good. After Black secures his stones with 9, White plays 10, attacking the two black stones at the top and strengthening his moyo on the right side.

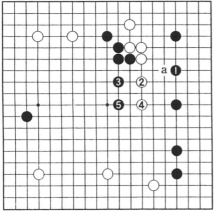

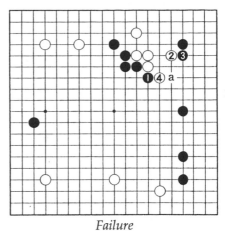

Problem 118. Correct Answer

Black should defend the right side with 1. White must escape with 2 and 4, but Black moves into the center with 3 and 5, pinning the white group against his stones on the right. Black 1 at 'a' would be an overplay.

Failure

Black 1 aims to confine White to the top, but he responds with 2 and 4, leaving Black without a good follow-up. If Black 3 at 'a', White will play at 3 and Black will be unable to put his thickness to good use.

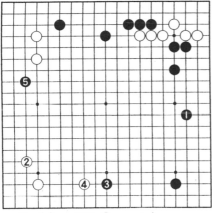

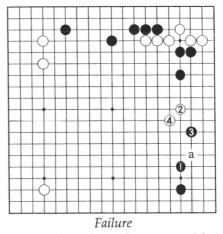

Problem 119. Correct Answer

Since it is a good idea to strengthen your weak stones, Black plays 1, the perfect move to defend his three stones in the upper right. It also works well with his stone below. The game continues to Black 5.

Failure

If Black encloses the corner with 1, White pincers with 2. Black 3 is a good move, but White 4 prevents the black stones above from linking up with their allies below. They must flee, so White gets the initiative.

Problem 120. White to Play

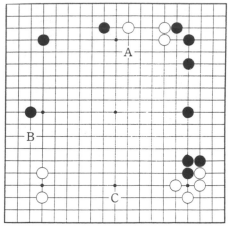

White has many good points to play, but there is one which takes precedence over all the others. Which of the three points indicated is best?

Problem 121. Black to Play

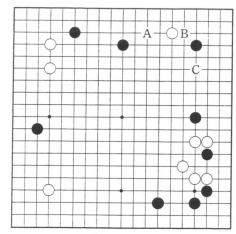

How should Black attack the lone white stone in the upper right: at A, B, or C?

Problem 122. Black to Play

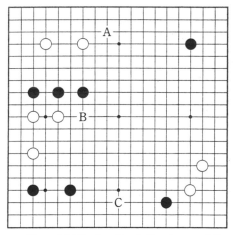

Should Black attack the two white stones at the top with A, attack the three white stones on the left side with B, or strengthen his position at the bottom with C?

Problem 123. Black to Play

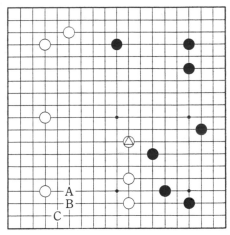

White has just played the marked stone, mapping out a huge moyo on the left, so the lower left is now the most important place to play. But where should Black play: at A, B, or C?

Problem 124. Black to Play

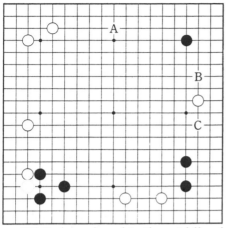

White has played in the middle of the right side. Should Black ignore this move and extend to A, or should he attack White with a move at B or C?

Problem 125. Black to Play

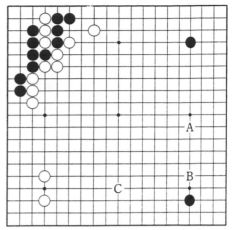

In the upper left corner, Black got profit while White made thickness. What is the best way for Black to counter this thickness?

Problem 126 Black to Play

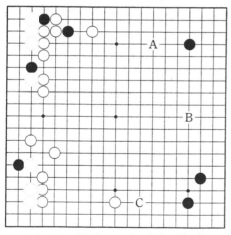

White is thick on the left side from the top to the bottom. Although Black has a lot of profit, he still has to prevent White from expanding the scale of his moyo. Where should he play?

Problem 127. White to Play

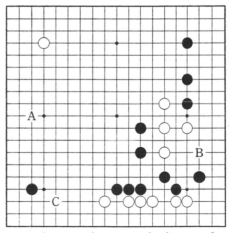

A sharp exchange took place on the lower right. It is White's move. Should he leave the right side as it is and play at A or C, or does he need to play a move at B?

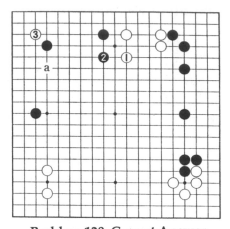

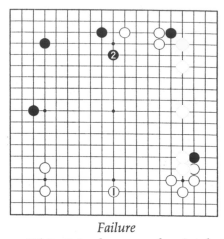

Problem 120. Correct Answer

White should strengthen his group by jumping to 1 and aim at invading the upper right and left corners. If Black 2, White 3 is the perfect invasion. Black could also play 2 at 'a'.

Failure

White 1 is also a good point, but Black 2 is a severe attack. White must escape, but then Black's moyos on both the left and the right will be strengthened.

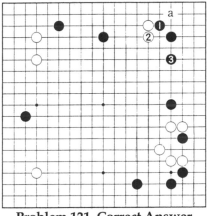

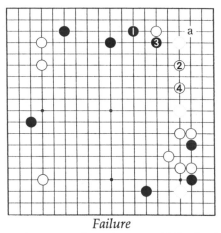

Problem 121. Correct Answer

Black 1 is a basic attacking move in this kind of position. When White stands at 2, Black jumps to 3. White's stones are now heavy and no matter how he defends, they will come under attack. If Black plays 1 at 3, White will slide to 'a' and secure his stone.

Failure

Against the pincer of Black 1, White will not invade at 'a'; instead, he will play 2 and 4, attacking the black stone in the middle of the right side.

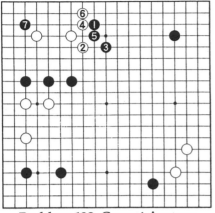

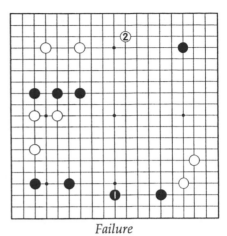

Problem 122. Correct Answer

The two white stones at the top are thin, so Black can take profit by attacking with the sequence to 5. After White 6, Black invades with 7. Because of the three black stones below, White's stones will be under a lot of pressure.

Failure

Black 1 is certainly a big point, but White 2 is even bigger. Black has lost his chance to seize the initiative at the top.

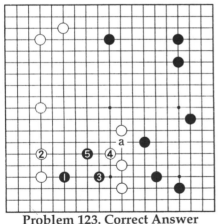

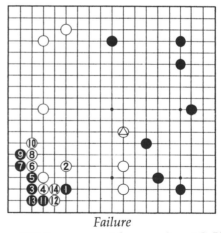

Problem 123. Correct Answer

Black should approach high with 1. If White 2, Black extends to 3, aiming to exploit the thinness of White's two-space jump by attaching at 'a'. White will defend at 4, but Black plays 5, wiping out much of White's moyo.

Failure

White answers 1 by capping at 2. If Black invades the corner with 3, after the sequence to 14, the marked stone makes a huge moyo with White's other stones on the left. If Black 1 at 12, White makes a bigger moyo with 1.

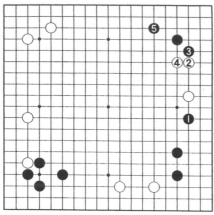

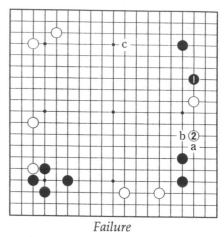

Problem 124. Correct Answer

Attacking the white stone with 1, driving it toward the star-point stone above, is best. White will extend to 2. The sequence to 5 is a joseki. If Black extends along the top, White will make a two-space extension down the right, attacking the black stones below.

Failure

Black 1 is in the wrong direction. White plays 2, aiming at Black's weak underbelly. The exchange of Black 'a' for White 'b' strengthens White, so it is not good. If Black defends his corner at the top, White makes a double-wing formation in the upper left with 'c'.

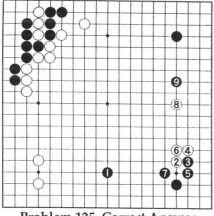

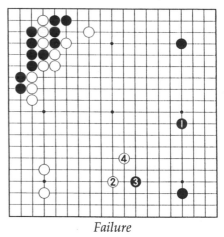

Problem 125. Correct Answer

Black 1 reduces the power of White's thickness. If White approaches with 2, Black plays the joseki to 7, taking profit in the lower right. After 9, Black is ahead in territory.

Failure

Black makes the Chinese-opening formation with 1, but White gets a chance to take the vital point of 2. If Black now plays 3, White plays 4 and a huge moyo emerges in the center.

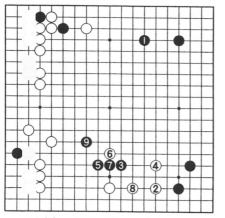

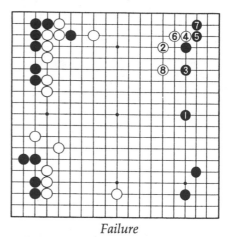

Problem 126. Correct Answer

Black 1 blocks White from making a large-scale moyo at the top while taking territory. Locally, Black 1 at 8 is big, but it is too dangerous to let White play at 1. If White answers 1 with 2, Black is satisfied with erasing White's moyo with the sequence to 9.

Failure

Black 1 is not good because it lets White make an approach move at 2. After the sequence to 8, White has made a huge moyo at the top.

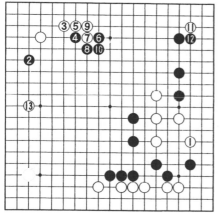

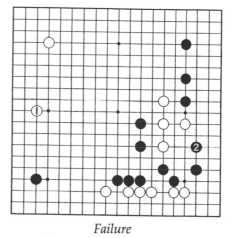

Problem 127. Correct Answer

Before anything else, White must secure his position on the lower right by playing on the urgent point of 1. The sequence to 13 is one possible continuation.

Failure

If White plays on the left side with 1 or approaches the stone in the lower left, Black will play 2, robbing White's stones of their base. These stones will now come under a severe attack.

Problem 128. White to Play

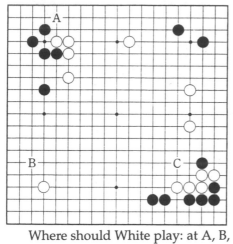

Where should White play: at A, B, or C?

Problem 129. White to Play

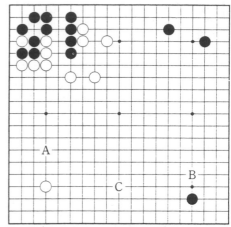

Taking into account White's position in the upper left, where do you think White should play?

Problem 130. Black to Play

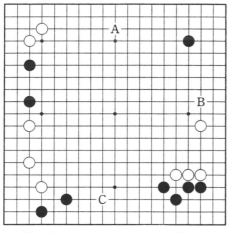

The biggest moves are the ones that have big follow-ups. Where do you think Black should play in this position?

Problem 131. Black to Play

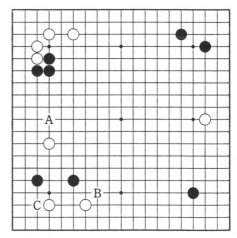

Before pincering the white stone on the left side, does Black need to make any preparatory moves? Of course, Black would like to finish up on the left side in sente so he can play on the right side before White.

Problem 132. White to Play

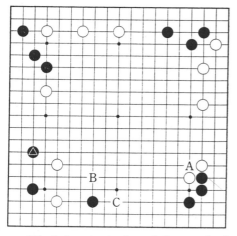

Black has just played the marked stone. Should White aggressively follow up with B or C, or should he calmly connect at A?

Problem 133. White to Play

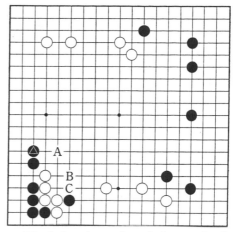

Black has just played the marked stone. In this position, which of the three points indicated is the best way for White to defend?

Problem 134. Black to Play

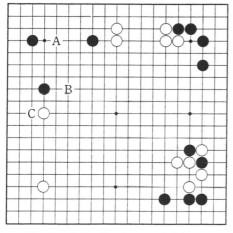

The joseki in the lower right corner has ended in sente for Black. He must now turn his attention to his thin position at the top. Where should he play?

Problem 135. Black to Play

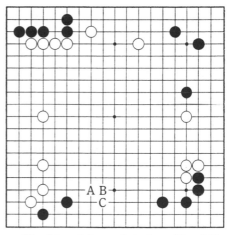

Black has taken a lot of profit, while White is staking the game on influence. It is now urgent for Black to play at the bottom, but which of the three points indicated should he play?

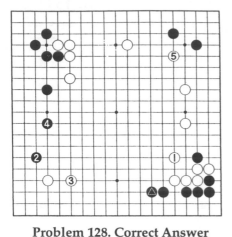

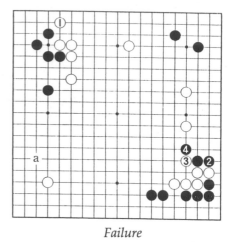

Problem 128. Correct Answer

In response to the marked stone, White 1 is the proper move. As expected, Black plays 2 and 4, but White will cap at 5, and suddenly a white moyo emerges in the center.

Failure

Locally, both White 1 and White 'a' are big moves, but if Black is allowed to play 2 and 4, the right side could be thrown into confusion.

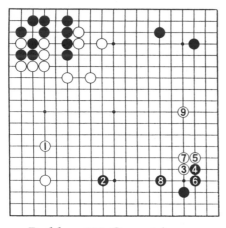

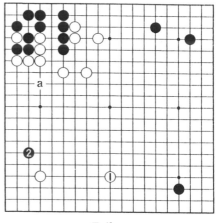

Problem 129. Correct Answer

White should extend to 1, making a moyo on the left side. This enables Black to take the good point at 2, but White can approach with 3 and, after the joseki to White 9, Black is unable to make a moyo on the right side.

Failure

White 1 is a big extension, but it is premature. Black can approach at 2, as well as force with 'a', so White's moyo strategy will have failed.

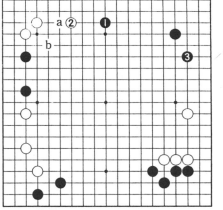

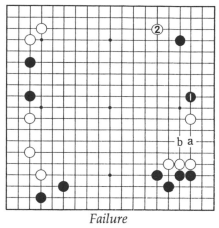

Problem 130. Correct Answer

Black 1 is a big move because it threatens 'a'. Next, Black would play 'b', and a moyo would begin to form in the center. This is not to White's liking, so he counters by extending to 2. But Black plays 3 and he gets a strong position in the upper right.

Failure

Black 1 aims at an invasion at 'a', but this is not much of a threat, since White 'b' would be an adequate response. Therefore, White will seize the initiative and make an approach move at 2.

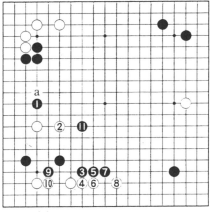

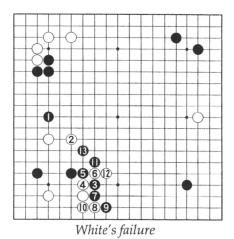

Problem 131. Correct Answer

Black must first play 1. When White jumps to 2, Black can force with the sequence to 9, then cap at 11. If Black 1 at 3, White will play 4 to 6, then extend to 'a'.

White's failure

In response to Black 3, White must not cut through with 4 and 6. After Black 13, White will find himself in a severe fight. (See Problem 151 in *Get Strong at Joseki 1*.)

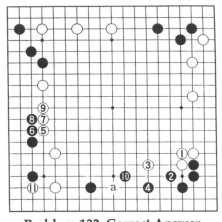

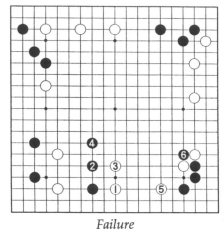

Problem 132. Correct Answer

White should connect at 1, then force Black to play 4 with 3 after Black 2. Next, White links up with his lone stone at the top with the sequence to 9. White now threatens an invasion at 'a', so Black must defend at 10.

Failure

White 1 and 3 are aggressive moves, but Black gets to cut at 6 after 5. White's stones are now scattered throughout the board and he lacks a unified strategy.

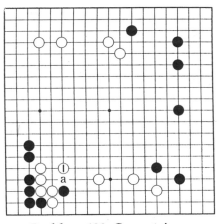

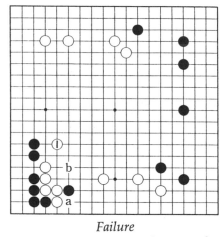

Problem 133. Correct Answer

White 1 is the correct shape here. It is more efficient than playing at 'a'.

Failure

White 1 is a large-scale move, but unfortunately Black 'a' or 'b' could be quite annoying for White later on.

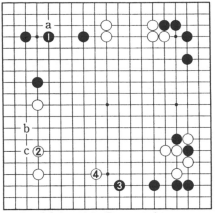

Problem 134. Correct Answer

Even though Black's position at the top is open from the right, he must make a corner enclosure at 1 and not at 'a'. Next, he can aim at 'b' or 'c', so White defends with 2. In response to Black 3, White 4 is a good move.

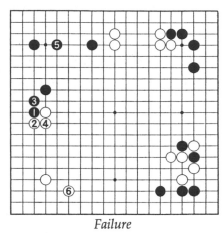

Failure

Black 1 and 3 are not good because they strengthen White's position on the left. This is a big loss for Black.

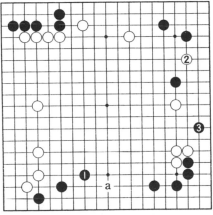

Problem 135. Correct Answer

Black 1 on the fourth line makes a good high-low balance with his stone on the right. An invasion at 'a' remains, but this would cause White's moyo on the left to be reduced. If White 2, Black will invade at 3.

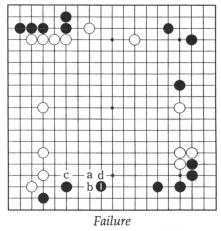

Failure

Black 1 is too low. Later, White can force with the sequence White 'a'– Black 'b'–White 'c', expanding his moyo on the left. Black 1 at 'd' is bad shape.

Problem 136. Black to Play

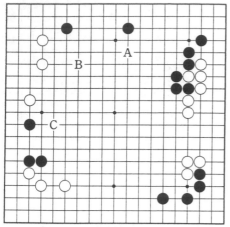

In this position, White has profit while Black has a moyo at the top. However, the black stones on the lower left are not very strong. How should Black continue?

Problem 137. White to Play

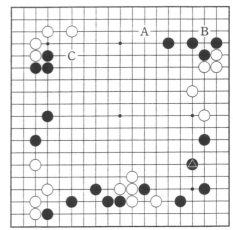

After Black plays the marked stone, the only interesting points remaining are at the top. Does White have any special strategem at B or is there something else he should do?

Problem 138. White to Play

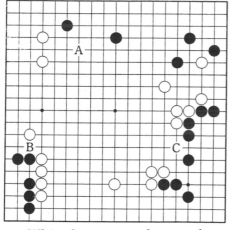

White has mapped out a huge moyo at the bottom. How should he now play?

Problem 139. Black to Play

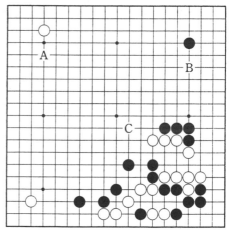

The proverb instructs us to play the urgent point before the big point. But sometimes it is hard to tell which points are urgent or even how urgent is it. Where is the urgent point here?

Problem 140. White to Play

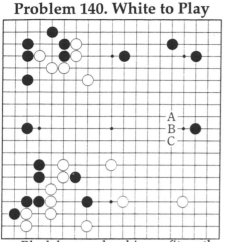

Black has made a big profit on the left side and has mapped out a moyo on the right, so it is urgent for White to reduce this moyo, but which point should he play: A, B, or C?

Problem 141. Black to Play

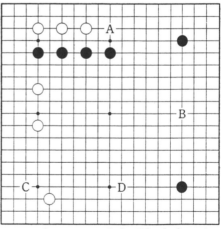

At the beginning of the game, you have to play the best move or your opponent may seize the initiative. Where is Black's biggest move?

Problem 142. White to Play

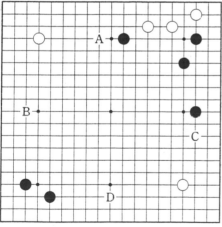

A joseki has just been played out in the upper right. How should White continue? Should he play an attacking move or should he be satisfied just taking a big point?

Problem 143. Black to Play

In the upper left, Black has invested a lot of stones to attack White, but his four stones there aren't taking any territory and he seems to be falling behind. Where should he play to rectify the balance of territories.

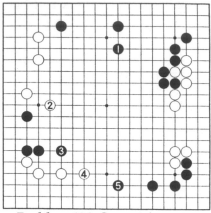

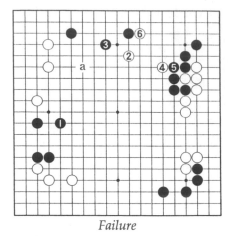

Problem 136. Correct Answer

Black should strengthen his position at the top with 1. White attacks with 2, but Black simply jumps to 3 and, after White 4, Black 5 is a big extension, aiming to slide under White's position on the left.

Failure

Black strengthens his position with 1 and prepares to attack the top and bottom. But White wipes out Black's moyo with the sequence from 2 to 6. If Black 1 at 'a', White could easily invade this moyo.

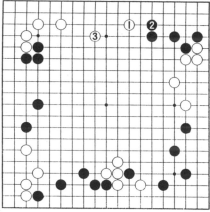

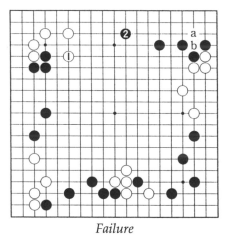

Problem 137. Correct Answer

The are no special tricks that White can pull off in the corner, so it is best for him to play 1, forcing Black to defend at 2. He can then take up a position at the top with 3. The middle game now begins.

Failure

A move like 1 does nothing to improve White's position. Black strengthens his weak stones at the top and takes profit besides. If White now peeps at 'a', Black simply connects at 'b' and the stone at 'a' is lost.

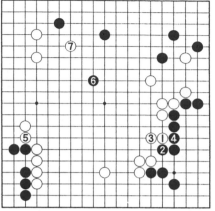

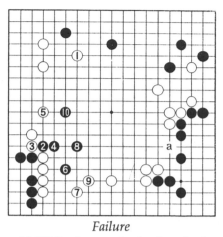

Problem 138. Correct Answer

Before doing anything else, White should peep at 1. Black must defend with 2 and 4 or else White will wipe out Black's territory on the right. Next, White protects his weakness at 5. If Black 6, White plays 7.

Failure

If White jumps to 1, threatening Black's territory at the top, Black will cut through with 2 and wipe out White's moyo with the sequence to 10. (See *Get Strong at Joseki 3*, Problems 153, 158, 163, and 168.)

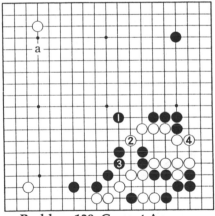

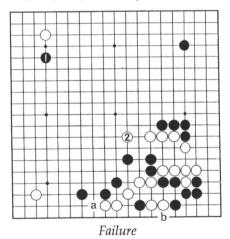

Problem 139. Correct Answer

It is important for Black to play 1 because it not only confines White to the right side, but also forces him to make life for his stones by descending to 4. After this, Black is free to play the big point at 'a' and take a big lead.

Failure

If Black rushes to play 1, White will jump to 2. If Black makes shape by forcing with 'a', White lives in sente with 'b', so Black 'a' is not a forcing move. As you can now see, the black stones at the bottom are vulnerable.

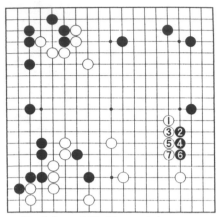

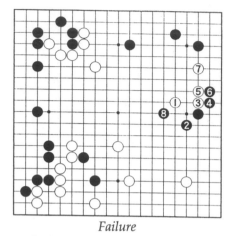

Problem 140. Correct Answer

White expands his moyo with 1 while limiting the size of Black's. Even though Black gains some profit up to 6, the scale of White's moyo is enough to maintain the balance of territories.

Failure

If White plays 1, Black will respond with 2 and, with the sequence to 8, White's moyo has been greatly reduced and his stones in the upper right are under attack.

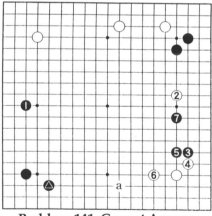

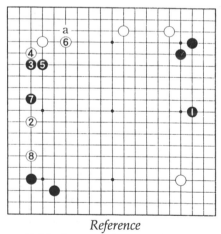

Problem 141. Correct Answer

Black 1, extending from his corner enclosure below, is the most effective move. Since the marked stone is on the third line, Black's position at the bottom would be too low if he played 1 at 'a'. The game continued with the sequence to Black 7.

Reference

If Black extends to 1, White will switch to the left side with 2 and, after the sequence to White 8, the value of Black's corner enclosure is diminished. Approaching inside White's sphere of influence with 1 at 'a' is not good at this early stage of the fuseki.

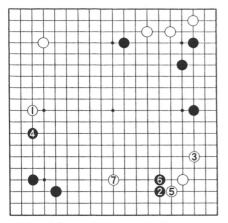

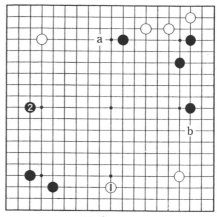

Problem 142. Correct Answer

White should extend to 1, limiting the influence of Black's corner enclosure. The game continued with the sequence to White 7. If Black neglects to extend to 4 and plays at 7 instead, White will extend down the left side.

Reference

White 1 is not good because Black can make an ideal extension from his corner enclosure with 2. White 'a' or 'b' are the next biggest points, but 1 and 2 take priority because no stones have been played in these areas yet.

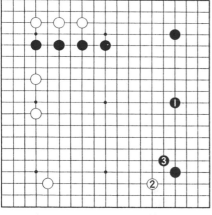

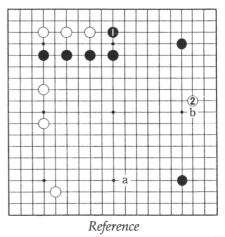

Problem 143. Correct Answer

Black should make a *sanren-sei* on the right with 1, aiming to make a moyo. In the game, Black answered the approach move at 2 with the diagonal move of 3.

Reference

The scale of Black 1 is too small. Also, it is not a serious threat against the white group, so White plays on the right with 2, preventing Black from making a large-scale moyo. If Black 1 at 'a', White will play 'b'.

Problem 144. White to Play

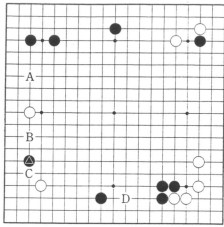

Black has played the marked stone, separating the white stones on the left. Black has strong positions above and below, so attacking this stone is not a good idea. Where should White play?

Problem 145. White to Play

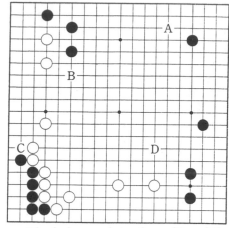

Black has a lot of profit, while White has thickness in the center. However, Black is also threatening to build a moyo in the center. Where should White play in this position?

Problem 146. White to Play

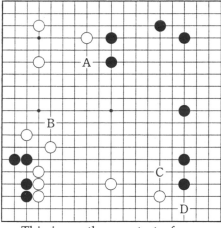

This is another contest of moyos. Where is the crucial point for White to play in this position?

Problem 147. Black to Play

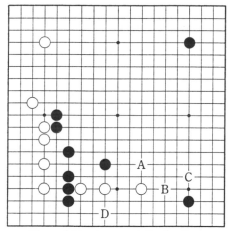

The white stones at the bottom are weak, so Black must find a good way to attack them. Note that Black gave White territory on the left in order to get a thick position in the center.

Problem 148. White to Play

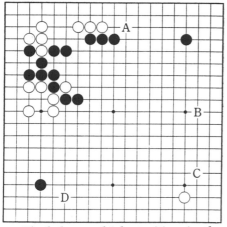

Black has a thick position in the upper left, but in compensation White has made profit at the top. White has sente and he would like to use it to get the most out of this position. Where should he play?

Problem 149. White to Play

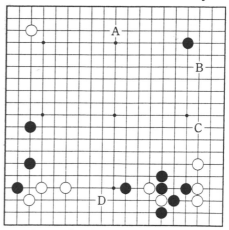

The joseki played in the lower right corner has ended in sente for White. There seem to be a lot of big points for him to play, but which one is the biggest?

Problem 150. White to Play

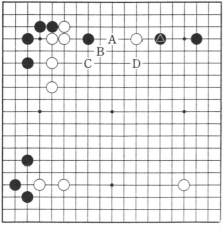

Black has just played the marked stone. How should White take control of the situation at the top?

Problem 151. White to Play

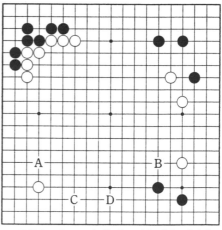

White is satisfied with his thickness in the upper left. However, he would like to use this thickness to build a moyo. Where should he play?

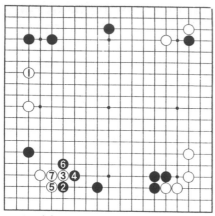

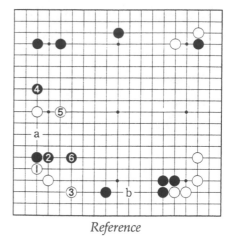

Problem 144. Correct Answer

White should extend to 1, strengthening his weakest stone. Next, Black will approach with 2 and White responds by attaching with 3. After 7, all of White's stones are secure.

Reference

If White defends his corner with 1 and 3, the white stone on the side will come under attack when Black extends from his corner enclosure with 4. After 6, Black has taken the lead.

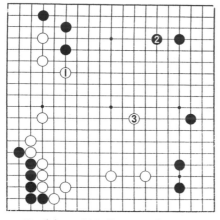

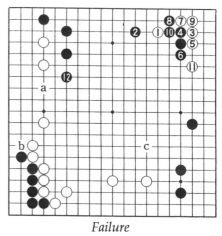

Problem 145. Correct Answer

Capping with White 1 is the biggest move. If Black defends the upper right with 2, White will stake out a vast moyo and wait for Black to try to invade it.

Failure

Against White 1, Black pincers with 2 and White must invade with 3. But, after 11, Black jumps to 12, aiming at 'a', so White must defend. White 1 at 'b' is big, but gote. White 1 at 'c' is another moyo focal point, but Black 2 at 12 leaves White's moyo wide open.

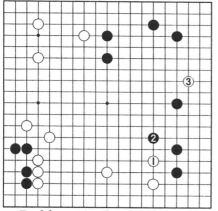

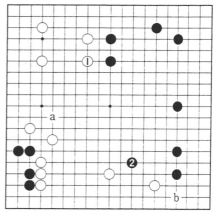

Problem 146. Correct Answer

White 1 is the biggest point. If Black caps with 2, White will switch to the upper right, invading with 3; he should have no trouble making a living group there.

Failure

White 1 is too narrow; the bottom is bigger, so Black will jump out to 2. White 1 at 'a' is only a defensive move. White 1 at 'b' only seeks territory: Black will ignore it and jump to 2.

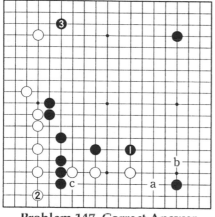

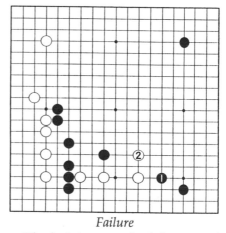

Problem 147. Correct Answer

Black should play a large-scale move by capping with 1. If White responds with 'a', Black 'b' has a good feel to it. White 2 is a good move because it prepares for White 'c', which threatens to link up or help his group at the center bottom make eyes.

Failure

Black 1 is very bad because it drives White into the center, compromising Black's thickness there.

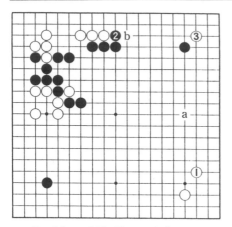

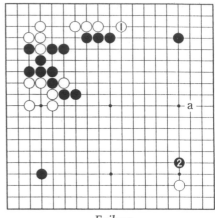

Problem 148. Correct Answer

White goes for territory by making a corner enclosure with 1. If Black turns at 2, White invades the corner with 3. If Black 2 at 'a', White will jump to 'b'.

Failure

White 1 is a big move, but Black will approach at 2. If White 1 at 'a', Black will again play 2. White's stones will then be scattered and lack unity, so Black would now be able to utilize his thickness by attacking them.

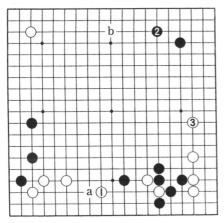

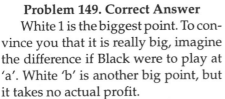

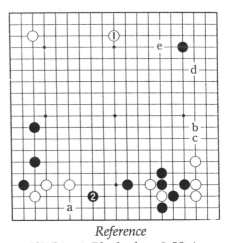

Problem 149. Correct Answer

White 1 is the biggest point. To convince you that it is really big, imagine the difference if Black were to play at 'a'. White 'b' is another big point, but it takes no actual profit.

Reference

If White 1, Black plays 2. He is now threatening to slide to 'a', uprooting the white stones there. White 1 at 'b' defends against Black 'c'. If White 1 at 'd', Black will jump to 'e', and another move on the side becomes necessary.

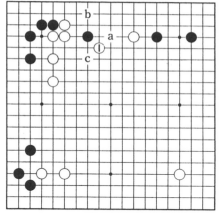

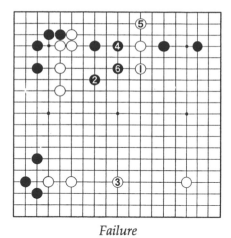

Problem 150. Correct Answer

White should play the shoulder hit of 1. Black will now find it hard to escape with his stone at the top. If White plays 1 at 'a', Black jumps down to 'b', threatening to link up to his stones on the left, then jumps to 'c'. If White 1 at 'c', Black can jump to 'a'.

Failure

White plays on a large scale when he jumps to 1, but when Black jumps out into the center with 2, White finds his stones at the top split apart. White plays 3 to restore the territorial balance, but Black secures his stones with 4 and 6. White has a lost game.

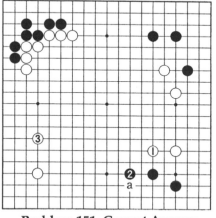

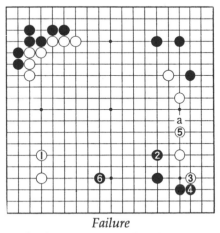

Problem 151. Correct Answer

Since the right side is thin, White should first strengthen it by jumping to 1. Next, White 3 starts to build a moyo on the left side. Black 2 at 'a' is bad because it is too low.

Failure

If White prematurely plays on the left with 1, Black will jump to 2, aiming at an invasion at 'a'. After extending to 6, Black's positions on both the right and left sides have been settled.

Problem 152. White to Play

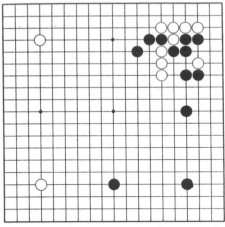

Both White and Black have weak stones in the center. How should White continue?

Problem 153. White to Play

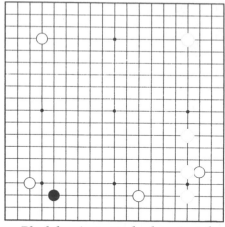

Black has just attached against the white stone on the lower right side. How should White respond?

Problem 154. Black to Play

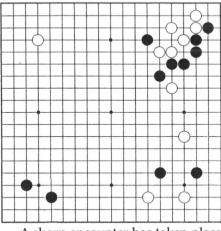

A sharp encounter has taken place in the upper right. Black's stones are out into the center and he would like to play a big extension on the left. Should Black do this immediately or should he make another move on the right?

Problem 155. Black to Play

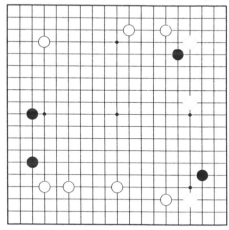

Kobayashi Koichi used to play the black formation on the right. Where should Black play next?

Problem 156. White to Play

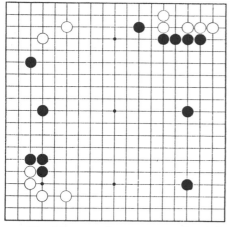

Black has made a moyo on the right with his *sanren-sei* formation, but there is still a weak point in his position. Where should White play next?

Problem 157. White to Play

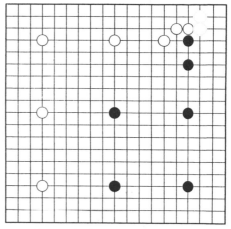

When Black occupies the central star point, he has staked out a huge moyo in the lower right. How should White counter it?

Problem 158. White to Play

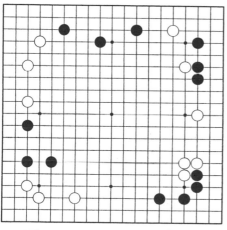

White's two stones in the upper right are floating without a base. How should White strengthen them?

Problem 159. Black to Play

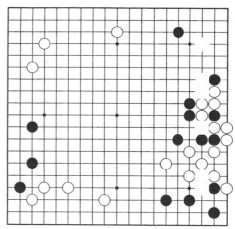

The fuseki has ended and the middle game has begun. Black has made a thick wall on the right. What is the best way for him to utilize this wall?

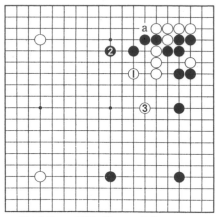

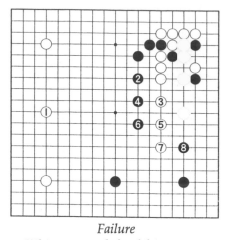

Problem 152. Correct Answer

White should force once with 1 then jump to 3, reducing the potential of Black's moyo at the bottom. White's stones are now in no danger. Black could also play 2 at 'a', but White's stones in the corner are safe, so he could just ignore it.

Failure

White must defend his stones on the right. If he makes a *sanren-sei* on the left with 1, Black will go on the offensive with the sequence from 2 to 8. Black has secured territory on the right, made influence in the center, and White's stones are in big trouble.

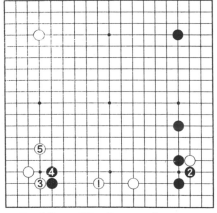

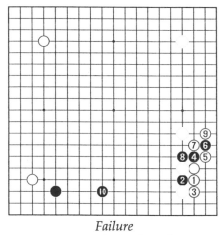

Problem 153. Correct Answer

White should extend to 1. This move is both a pincer and an extension. If Black secures the corner with 2, White goes on the attack with 3 and 5.

Failure

It is not a good idea for White to try to live in the corner. Black builds a thick wall with the sequence to 8 and, after White 9, Black pincers with 10, making a moyo at the bottom.

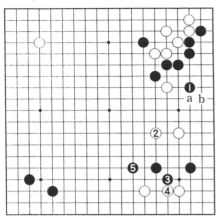

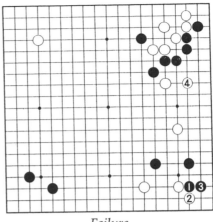

Problem 154. Correct Answer

Black 1 is the most urgent point. This move makes Black's stones in the upper right absolutely safe and it also takes away space for White to make his own stones safe. If White jumps to 2, Black forces with 3, then jumps to 5. White is still under attack. If White 2 at 'a', Black will play at 'b'.

Failure

If Black makes a base for his stones in the lower right with 1, White will exchange 2 for Black 3, then secure his stones on the right side with 4. The black stones above are still insecure and the game now favors White.

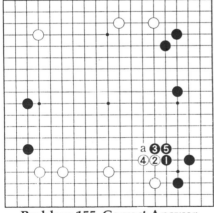

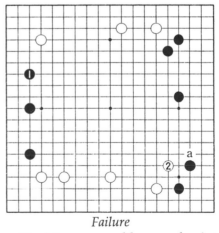

Problem 155. Correct Answer

Black should jump to 1, aiming to attack White at the bottom. White must defend. If he attaches at 2, Black makes a moyo on the right with 3 and 5. Black 5 at 'a' is also a strong move.

Failure

Black 1 may seem like a good point, but White will press at 2, wiping out Black's moyo. Next, White 'a' would be a severe move.

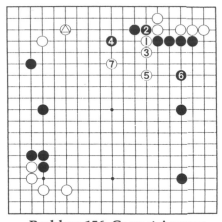

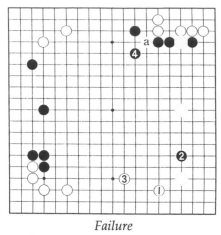

Problem 156. Correct Answer

Cutting through the black position with 1 and 3 is the standard follow-up to this joseki. It is particularly effective here because White has the marked stone in place, making White 7 a severe move.

Failure

If White approaches with 1 at the bottom, Black simply answers with 2. White completes the sequence with 3, letting Black defend against the threat of White 'a' with 4. Black is satisfied with this result.

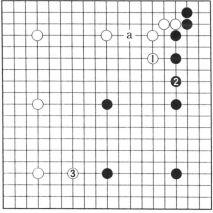

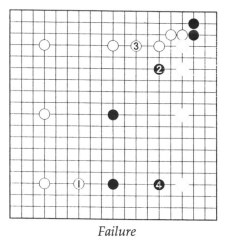

Problem 157. Correct Answer

White should jump to 1. This move defends White's weak point at 'a', forces Black to defend at 2, and expands White's moyo at the top. White can now extend to 3.

Failure

It is premature to play White 1 without any preparation. Black will jump to 2, forcing White to defend with 3. Now Black solidifies his moyo with 4.

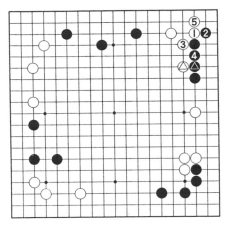

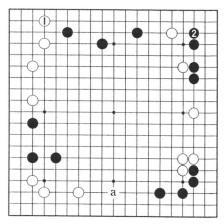

Problem 158. Correct Answer

Since White exchanged the marked stones before attaching at 1, Black is now forced to follow the joseki with 2 and 4. After descending to 5, White has made a base for his stones. All his groups are now safe.

Failure

Territorially, White 1 and White 'a' are big moves, but Black will descend at 2 and the two white stones are left floating in the center without a base. Before any other move, White 1 at 2 is absolutely essential.

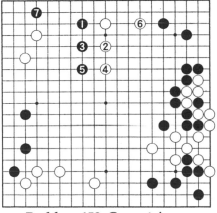

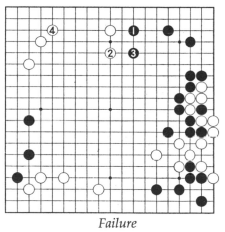

Problem 159. Correct Answer

Invading at 1 is the best way for Black to use his thickness. If White 2 and 4, Black keeps up the pressure with 3 and 5. White makes a base for his stones with 6, but Black slides to 7 and White is behind in territory.

Failure

Thickness should be used to attack. If Black tries to make territory with 1 and 3, White takes the lead with 2 and 4. The black stones on the right are now overconcentrated, while White's stones are taking territory efficiently.

Problem 160. White to Play

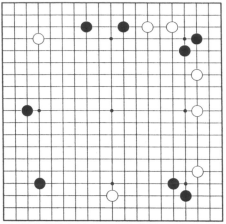

It is White's turn and if he plays the right move he can seize the initiative. Where should he play?

Problem 161. Black to Play

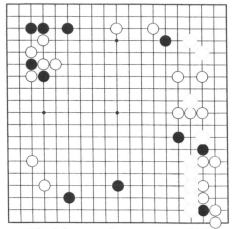

Black has made a moyo at the bottom that may need some tending to, but his three stones in the upper right corner are under siege. What should Black do?

Problem 162. White to Play

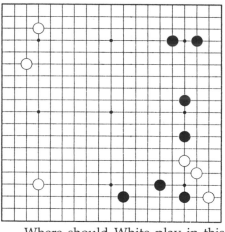

Where should White play in this position?

Problem 163. White to Play

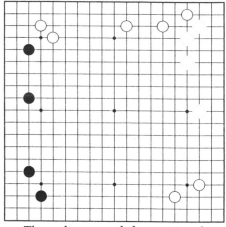

The only moves left are extensions along the side. Where should White play?

Problem 164. Black to Play

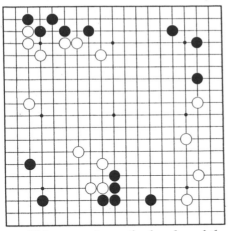

This game is on the border of the fuseki and the middle game. Now is Black's chance to seize the initiative. If he plays the right move, victory will be within his grasp.

Problem 165. Black to Play

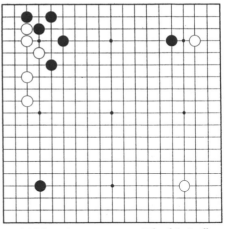

Taking into account Black's influence in the upper left, what is Black's strongest move?

Problem 166. Black to Play

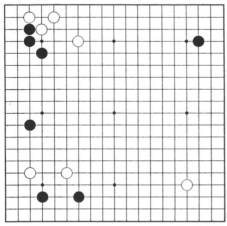

Black should be happy about his result on the left side. Can he now switch to the right side, or is there something else still remaining to be done on the left?

Problem 167. White to Play

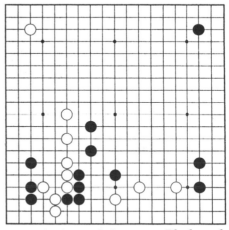

In the lower left corner, Black and White both advanced into the center. However, White ended in sente. How should he play now so as take control of the game?

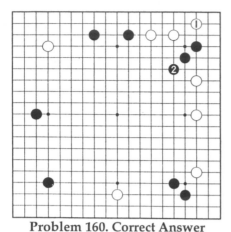

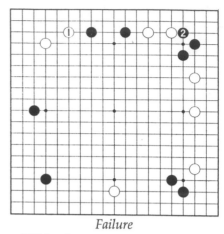

Problem 160. Correct Answer

White 1 is the vital point. With this move, White makes a base for his stone at the top left and deprives Black of a base for his. Therefore, Black must run away into the center with 2.

Failure

White 1 puts pressure on the two black stones at the top, but Black turns the tables on White by attaching with 2. Black has taken nearly 10 points of territory and the two white stones at the top are under attack.

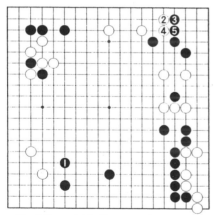

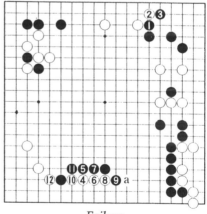

Problem 161. Correct Answer

Black must complete his moyo at the bottom by jumping to 1. The black stones at the top are not in great danger. The best White can do is to play 2 and 4, but Black secures a large corner with 3 and 5.

Failure

If Black defends the upper right corner with 1 and 3, White will invade with 4 and wipe out most of Black's moyo with the sequence to 12. This is a big loss for Black.

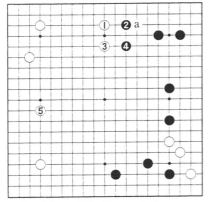

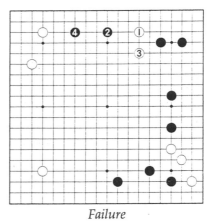

Problem 162. Correct Answer

White should extend to 1. If Black plays the checking extension of 2, White will exchange 3 for 4, then make a double-wing formation in the upper left. White's moyo is bigger in scale than Black's.

Failure

White 1 is an overplay. Black is strong on the right, so he can pincer at 2 and extend to 4 after 3. Black has stabilized his stones at the top, but White's are now floating in the center.

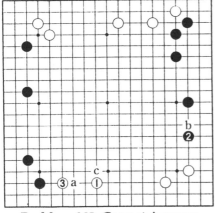

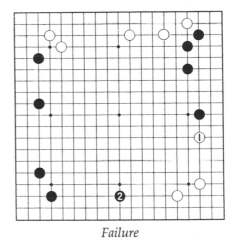

Problem 163. Correct Answer

White should extend all the way to 1. If Black 2, White can make a checking extension with 3. If Black 2 at 'a', White takes the last big extension at 'b'. White must not make a high extension to 'c' because Black 'a' threatens an invasion on the lower side.

Failure

The checking extension on the right side with 1 is not necessarily bad, but Black will extend to 2 and make an ideal double-wing formation from his corner enclosure in the lower left. For that reason, White 1 must be criticized.

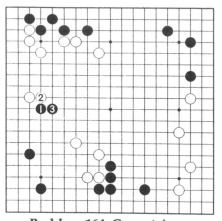

Problem 164. Correct Answer

The shoulder hit of Black 1 is the perfect point. It prevents the four stones at the bottom from joining up with their allies in the upper left to make a huge moyo in the center.

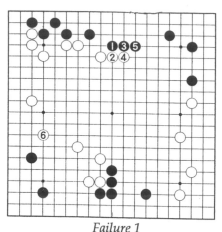

Failure 1

Locally, Black 1 at the top is a good move. However, White will push with 2 and 4, then play 6, making a deep moyo in the center.

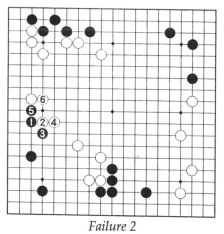

Failure 2

Although in the right direction, Black 1 is too low. White will attach with 2 and 4. After White 6, White has again made a large-scale moyo in the center.

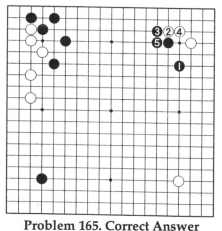

Problem 165. Correct Answer

Black should play at 1, making outside influence and restricting White to the corner. Against White 2 and 4, Black maps out a moyo at the top with 3 and 5.

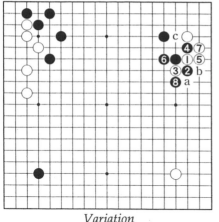

Variation

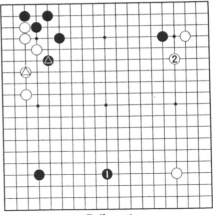

Failure 1

White could also attach on the right with 1. The sequence to Black 8 is a joseki. Since the ladder is favorable for Black, he is happy with this result. If White 7 at 'a', Black takes profit in the corner with the sequence Black 7–White 'b'–Black 'c'.

Extending to Black 1 at the bottom is not good. White will play 2 and stake out a claim on the right side. White 2 also inhibits the development of a black moyo at the top, so now the exchange of the marked black and white stones is not good for Black.

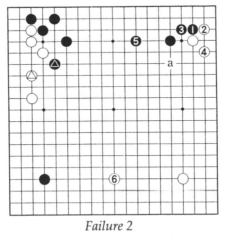

Failure 2

The sequence to White 4 is a joseki, but the extension of Black 5 is unsatisfactory because it doesn't make an efficient moyo with respect to the marked black stone on the left. Black 5 at 'a' certainly makes a moyo on a grand scale, but Black's position at the top is too thin to support it, so White will have an easy time invading it.

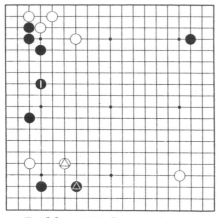

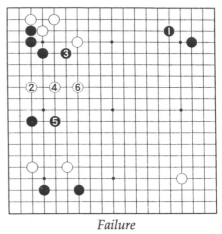

Problem 166. Correct Answer

Defending with Black 1 is the best move. This makes the exchange of the marked stones bad for White. White's two stones on the lower left are now caught between two strong black positions.

Failure

Making a corner enclosure with Black 1 is not good. Black's position on the left is too thin. White will invade with 2 and Black is left with two weak groups to defend after White 6.

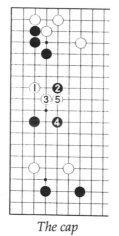

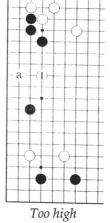

The cap

Black might try to counter White's invasion at 1 by capping with 2, but White simply moves out into the center with 3 and 5.

Too high

White 1 on the fourth line is too high. If Black's stones get into trouble, he can always link up at 'a'.

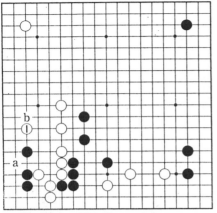

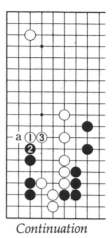

Problem 167. Correct Answer

White 1 is a strong move that takes control of the left side and threatens the black stones with a peep at 'a'. An extension to Black 'b' would be a very big move.

Continuation

Black has to defend his corner with 2, forcing White to strengthen his stones with 3. Instead of 3, White could also descend to 'a'.

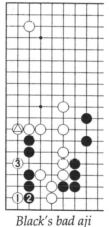

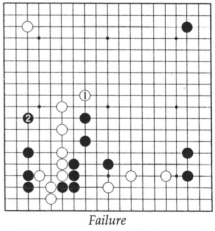

Black's bad aji

Descending with the marked stone is sente against the black stones in the corner. If Black ignores this move, White will play 1 and 3, and Black's stones are dead.

Failure

With respect to the black stones in the center, White 1 is certainly a big point, but Black will ignore it and extend to 2. There is a big difference between this diagram and the correct answer. Here, Black has expanded his territory on the left, leaving the white stones thin.

Problem 168. White to Play

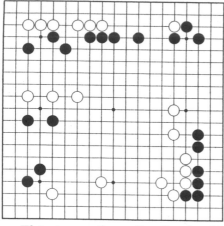

This is another after-the-fuseki problem. Where is the vital point for White to play?

Problem 169. Black to Play

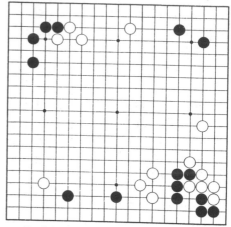

In this position it is urgent for Black to settle his stones in the lower right. Where should he play?

Problem 170. Black to Play

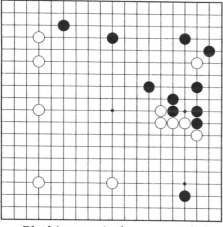

Black's moyo in the upper right has almost turned into sure territory. However, his stone in the lower right corner seems to have gotten left behind in the battle above. Black must not forsake this stone, but what is the best way to strengthen it?

Problem 171. Black to Play

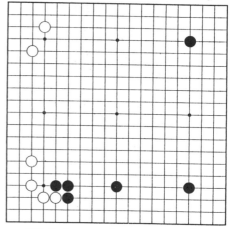

White has made a corner enclosure in the upper left corner. Where should Black now play?

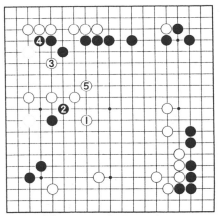

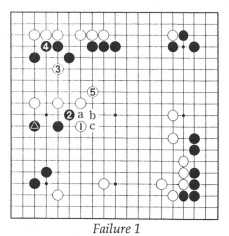

Problem 168. Correct Answer

The knight's move of Black 1 is the vital point. With this move, White builds a moyo in the center and Black is now unable to use his thick wall above to attack White. If Black peeps at 2, White defends by forcing with 3, then playing the diagonal move of 5.

Failure 1

There is a big difference between White 1 and the knight's move in the correct answer. The double peep of Black 2, anchored by his marked stone, is now a strong move. After 3 and 5, Black can cut through with the sequence Black 'a'–White 'b'–Black 'c'.

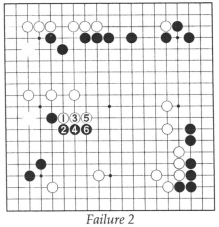

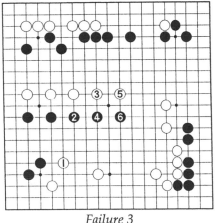

Failure 2

Attaching with 1 only helps Black to march into White's potential moyo with the sequence to 6.

Failure 3

Although White 1 is often a good move, in this case it is too small in scale. Black advances into White's sphere of influence with the sequence to 6 while using his thickness to maintain the pressure on White.

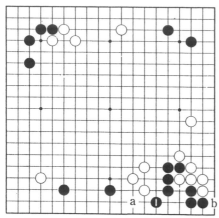

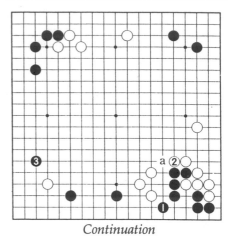

Problem 169. Correct Answer

Black should defend his stones with 1. Black doesn't have to worry about their safety anymore because he can either link up to his stones on the left with 'a' or make two eyes with 'b'.

Continuation

If White blocks with 2, Black is happy just to play the approach move of 3. Black is threatening to hane at 'a', so White cannot avoid a disadvantageous fight.

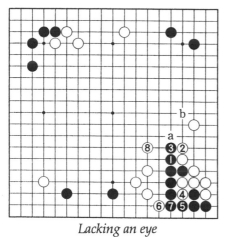

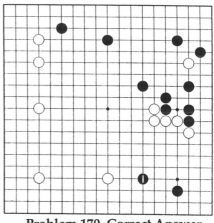

Lacking an eye

It might seem more natural for Black to prevent the blockade and advance into the center with 1 and 3, but White would force with 4 and 6. Black's group doesn't have two eyes and White goes on the attack with 8. If Black 'a' next, White will play at 'b'.

Problem 170. Correct Answer

Because White is thick above, Black should extend tightly with the large knight's move of 1. Black's stones at the bottom are now secure.

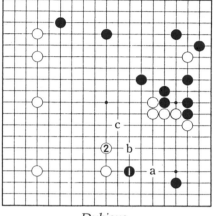

Dubious

Extending all the way to 1 leaves Black a bit thin. White will jump to 2, and Black will be troubled by the possibility of a white invasion at 'a'. If Black jumps to 'b' to strengthen his stones, White will play 'c', building up a moyo in the center.

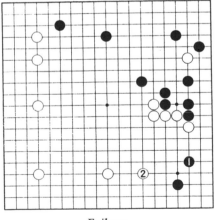

Failure

Making a corner enclosure with 1 is overly defensive. White now takes the strategic point of 2. Compare this diagram with the correct answer and you will understand why Black 1 is not an efficient move.

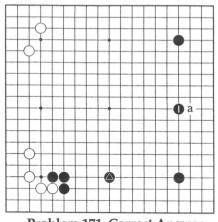

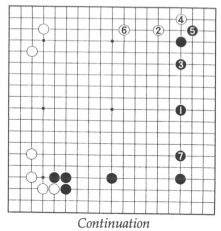

Problem 171. Correct Answer

Black should make a *sanren-sei* on the right side with 1. With the marked stone at the bottom, this moyo is like an eagle, spreading its great wings in flight. Black 1 at 'a' would be too low, as it would be open to a capping move.

Continuation

Next, White will approach with 2; the continuation to 6 is one possibility. At this point, Black will strengthen his position in the lower right with 7.

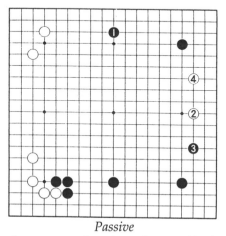

Passive

Black plays 1 in order to neutralize the influence of White's corner enclosure in the upper left corner, but this move is dubious. White will play 2 and 4 to stake out a position on the right side. Of course, we can't say that Black's position is bad, but it is going to be a long, hard game for him.

Problem 172. White to Play

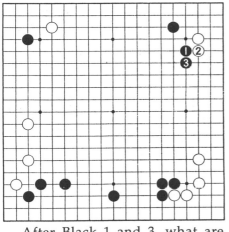

After Black 1 and 3, what are White's next two moves?

Problem 173. Black to Play

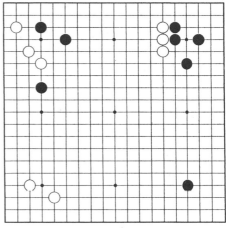

Black has to make an important defensive move. Where is it?

Problem 174. Black to Play

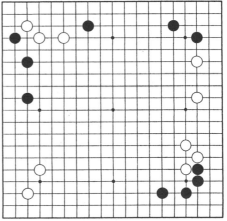

In this position, the first thing you should focus on is the group of three white stones on the left side. How should Black attack them?

Problem 175. Black to Play

There are a lot of points that Black might play, but he should focus on strengthening his position at the top. Where should he play?

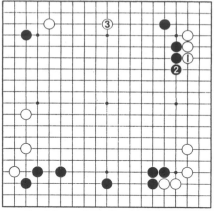

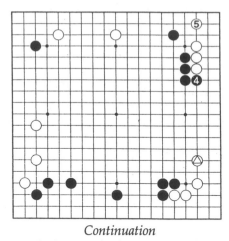

Problem 172. Correct Answer

White should crawl once with 1, then extend to 3 to neutralize Black's thick wall on the right.

Continuation

Black 4 is a thick move, but, in this case, White doesn't mind because his marked stone neutralizes this thickness. White next jumps to 5 in order to live in the corner.

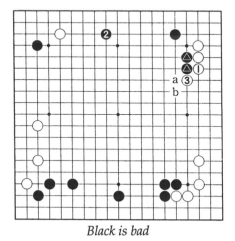

Black is bad

If Black ignores White 1 and pincers with 2, White will hane with 3. If Black also hanes at 'a', White will play a two-step hane at 'b' and the right side will have become big. In any case, the two marked black stones have become bad moves because they have given White profit. If Black wants to pincer with 2, he should do so without playing the marked stones.

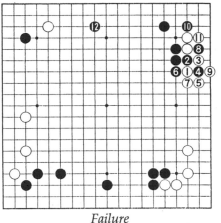

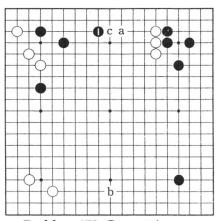

Failure

Jumping to White 1 is not good. Black will strengthen his position with the forcing moves to 10, then pincer with 12.

Problem 173. Correct Answer

White's three stones to the right are thick, so Black should extend tightly to 1. If White answers with 'a', Black will take the big point at 'b'. Black could also extend to 'c', but this is a bit too close to White's three thick stones, so his position at the top would be thin.

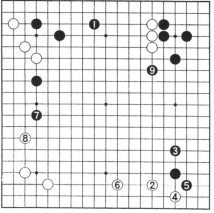

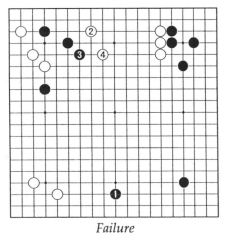

Continuation

After Black 1, White will probably switch to the lower right and play the joseki to 6. After exchanging 7 for 8, Black will attack the three white stones by capping with 9.

Failure

If Black doesn't defend at the top, but plays 1 instead, White will seize the initiative by attacking with 2. When Black runs away with 3, White makes territory at the top with 4.

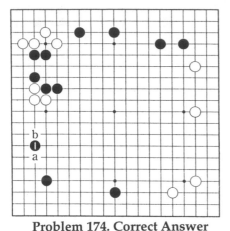

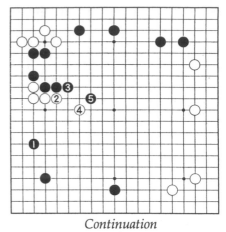

Problem 174. Correct Answer

Black 1 is the ideal point to attack the white stones. Black 1 at 'a' leaves room for a white extension to 'b'. Black 1 at 'b' would be too close to White's thick position above.

Continuation

In response to Black 1, White must run away with 2 and 4. While Black is chasing White, he is going to be building a moyo at the top and strengthening his stones in the lower left.

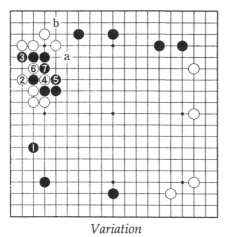

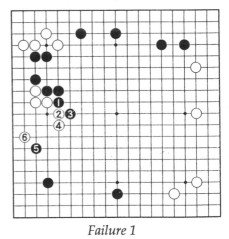

Variation

If White plays 2, the sequence to Black 7 would follow. After this, confining White with Black 'a' or sliding to Black 'b' would be a severe attack on the white stones.

Failure 1

Black 1 and 3 are in the wrong direction. Black must now extend with 5, but White settles his stones with 6.

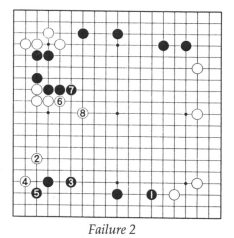

Failure 2

Black has to attack the white stones on the left. If he extends to 1 at the bottom right, White will approach with 2 and his stones on the left side will be settled.

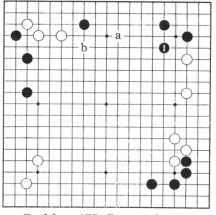

Problem 175. Correct Answer

Black 1 is the best point in this position, since it prevents White from expanding his own position on the right. Next, if White invades at 'a', Black will jump to 'b' and the white stones on the left, as well as the one at 'a', will come under attack.

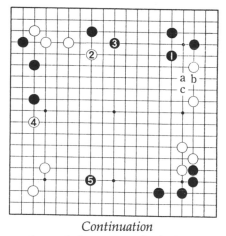

Continuation

One of the aims of Black 1 is to build influence with the sequence Black 'a'–White 'b'–Black 'c', so it is not a good idea for White to invade at the top. Therefore, he might exchange 2 for 3, then extend to 4. Black would then take the last big extension at 5.

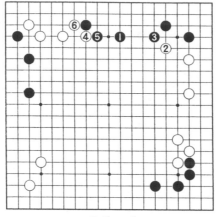

Failure 1

Black 1 is a rather dull move. White expands his moyo on the right while flattening Black with 2. He then defends his stones on the left with 4 and 6. Black 1 thinks only of defending his territory at the top.

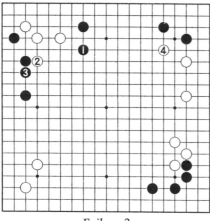

Failure 2

Black 1 also misses the point. White first forces with 2 to make sure that his stones on the left can escape, then plays the vital point of 4.

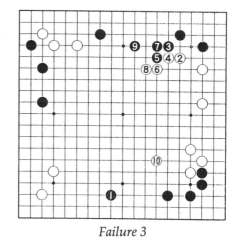

Failure 3

The top is most important in this position. If Black plays at the bottom with 1, White will expand his moyo on the right side with the sequence to 10.

Go Books from Kiseido

Get Strong at Go Series

A series of problem books covering every phase of the game from the opening to the endgame. Each book contains 170 or more problems ranging in difficulty from elementary to advanced. Thus, they can be used by players ranging in strength from 20-kyu to dan-level. By studying go in this problem format, you will not only learn basic principles as to why moves are made but also train yourself in thinking through and analyzing positions. You will encounter a great many of the same or similar patterns that will arise in your own games. We guarantee that diligent study of this entire series will lay the foundation for becoming a truly strong player.

K51: Volume 1: **Get Strong at the Opening**
K52: Volume 2: **Get Strong at Joseki I**
K53: Volume 3: **Get Strong at Joseki II**
K54: Volume 4: **Get Strong at Joseki III**
K55: Volume 5: **Get Strong at Invading**
K56: Volume 6: **Get Strong at Tesuji**
K57: Volume 7: **Get Strong at the Endgame**
K58: Volume 8: **Get Strong at Life and Death**
K59: Volume 9: **Get Strong at Handicap Go**
K60: Volume 10: **Get Strong at Attacking**

Other books on Go available from Kiseido

Introductory and General

K50: **Go — A Complete Introduction to the Game**, by Cho Chikun
K40: **The Go Player's Almanac 2001**, edited by Richard Bozulich

Problem Books for Beginners
Graded Go Problems for Beginners, by Kano Yoshinori
K46: Volumes 1, Introductory Problems (30-kyu to 25-kyu)
K47: Volumes 2, Elementary Problems (25-kyu to 12-kyu)
K48: Volumes 3, Intermediate Problems (12-kyu to 6-kyu)
K49: Volumes 4, Advanced Problems (6-kyu to 2-kyu)

Elementary Go Series

For more than 20 years, the Elementary Go Series has been the standard texts for go players who want to get a firm grasp of the fundamental of go. Not only is the theory of go elaborated on, the reader is also given problems to show how these theoretical concepts are applied in actual games.

K10: Volume 1: **In the Beginning — The opening in the Game of Go** by Ishigure Ikuro
K11: Volume 2: **38 Basic Joseki**, by Kosugi Kiyoshi and James Davies
K12: Volume 3: **Tesuji**, by James Davies
K13: Volume 4: **Life and Death**, by James Davies
K14: Volume 5: **Attack and Defense**, by Ishida Akira and James Davies
K15: Volume 6: **The Endgame**, by Ogawa Tomoko and James Davies
K16: Volume 7: **Handicap Go**, by Nagahara Yoshiaki and Richard Bozulich

Mastering the Basics

A series of books, especially written for high-kyu player, for mastering the basic techniques of go. Each book in this series consists of hundreds of problems designed to hammer home the fundamental concepts of go theory and technique. A thorough and patient study of this series is the fastest way to go through the kyu ranks.

K71: Volume 1: **501 Opening Problems**, by Richard Bozulich and Rob van Zeijst
K72: Volume 2: **1001 Life-and-Death Problems**, by Richard Bozulich
K73: Volume 3: **Making Good Shape**, by Rob van Zeijst and Richard Bozulich
K74: Volume 4: **501 Tesuji Problems,** by Richard Bozulich
Other volumes in this series are being planned.

Elementary Books

K02: **Basic Techniques of Go**, by Nagahara Yoshiaki and Haruyama Isamu
K31: **The Second Book of Go**, by Richard Bozulich
K17: **Kage's Secret Chronicles of Handicap Go**, by Kageyama Toshiro
K28: **Lessons in the Fundamentals of Go**, by Kageyama Toshiro

Intermediate Books

K26: **The Direction of Play**, by Kajiwara Takeo
K33: **The Chinese Opening — The Sure-Win Strategy**, by Kato Masao
K45: **Positional Judgment — High-Speed Game Analysis**, by Cho Chikun
K69: **Cosmic Go — A Guide to Four-Stone Handicap Games** by Sangit Chatterjee and Yang Huiren

Advanced Books
Dictionary of Basic Josekis, by Ishida Yoshio
K21: Volume 1 — 3–4 Point Josekis
K22: Volume 2 — 3–5 Point Josekis
K23: Volume 3 — 5–4 and 4–4 Point Josekis
K29: **Reducing Territorial Frameworks,** by Fujisawa Shuko
K81: **A Survey of Modern Openings**

Game Collections

K01: **Invincible: The Games of Shusaku,** edited and compiled by John Power
K07: **The 1971 Honinbo Tournament,** by Iwamoto Kaoru
K25: **Appreciating Famous Games,** by Ohira Shuzo
PP01: **Tournament Go 1992,** edited and compiled by John Power

Go World
A quarterly magazine covering the Chinese, Korean and Japanese tournament scene. Instructional articles for beginners to advanced players.

North America
Kiseido, 2255 - 29th Street, Suite 4
Santa Monica, CA 94903-3618;
Tel: 1-800-988-6463; FAX 1-310-578-7381;
e-mail: sales@kiseido.com   *http://www.kiseido.com*

Europe
Schaak en Gowinkel het Paard, Haarlemmerdijk 147
1013 KH Amsterdam, Holland; e-mail: paard@xs4all.nl
Tel: +31-20-624-1171; FAX: +31-20-627-0885.

Direct from Japan
Kiseido Publishing Company, CPO Box 1140, Tokyo, Japan.
FAX +81-467-57-5814
e-mail: kiseido@yk.rim.or.jp;   *http://www.kiseido.com*

A free catalog and price list of books and go equipment are available by writing to one of the following companies.

Play Go Online Using

KISEIDO GO SERVER (KGS)

You can now play go online through the **Kiseido Go Server (KGS)**. It can be accessed through Kiseido's home page at **http://www.kiseido.com**, or you can go to it directly at **http://kgs.kiseido.com**. There is no charge for playing games on this site, and this server works for Linux/Unix, Mac, and Windows.

The Kiseido Go Server has the following features not found on any other go server.

1. On the **Kiseido Go Server**, you can edit games online.

2. The **Kiseido Go Server** is multilingual. All messages that players type and send are done in Unicode, which means that people can converse in any language that they wish.

3. The **Kiseido Go Server** is the only go server that truly supports Japanese scoring. It also supports Chinese rules, AGA (American) rules, and the New Zealand rule sets.

4. With the **Kiseido Go Server** you can play with no time limit, with an absolute time limit, or with various byo-yomi systems.

5. The **Kiseido Go Server** also allows you to save and retrieve your games free of charge, enabling you to review and study them later.

We at Kiseido hope to meet you on the **Kiseido Go Server** at:

http://kgs.kiseido.com